OFF CRACK AND BACK ON TRACK

OFF CRACK AND BACK ON TRACK

Written By:

Karey Russell
&
Evangelist Myra Pratt

Copyright © 2013 by Karey Russell & Evangelist Myra Pratt.

Library of Congress Control Number: 2013905472
ISBN: Hardcover   978-1-4836-1607-0
              Softcover   978-1-4836-1606-3
              Ebook   978-1-4836-1608-7

All rights reserved. No part of this book may be reproduced or transmitted in any form or by any means, electronic or mechanical, including photocopying, recording, or by any information storage and retrieval system, without permission in writing from the copyright owner.

This book was printed in the United States of America.

Rev. date: 04/27/13

To order additional copies of this book, contact:
Xlibris Corporation
1-888-795-4274
www.Xlibris.com
Orders@Xlibris.com
130374

CONTENTS

1

I) The Early Years 13
II) The Separation..19
III) Life with Addicts..22
IV) The Desire to Change 32
V) The True Way 37

2

I) Introduction to Crack 39
II) I did it For Crack 42
III) All Cracked Out 45
IV) No Rescuer 49
V) Three Marriages...52
VI) In Harm's Way 61
VII) Getting Money for Crack..67
VIII) Driven by Crack 70
IX) A Victim of Rape 72
X) Prison Time 79
XI) Bad Relationships 82
XII) The Power to Overcome 86

DEDICATION

This Story is dedicated to
My two daughters Karey and Coretta.
They are the tool that
God used to bring me back
From the depths of hell and drug addiction.
My mother raised me in the church.
But as I got older, Satan
Took my hand and I followed him to
The door of death and destruction.
The devil comes to kill, steal, and to destroy
but Jesus came to give us life and life more abundantly.
To understand my praise
You need to know my story.

Special Thanks to:

Connie Baker-Smith
Eleanor Hollands
Vallie Pratt
Dr. Louise Lyas

It's 2013 and I'm ten years clean.

Thank You Jesus

"Isn't God Good?"

FORWARD

I asked my mother to share her stories with me of her life as a crack cocaine addict. She tells how it affected her life and I tell how it affected mine. All the stories in this book are true and depict the devastation of crack addiction.

I

The Early Years

MY NAME IS Karey Lee Russell. I was born January 14, 1974 to Leotis Crawford and Myra Pratt Crawford. Two and a half years later my sister Coretta Lynn Crawford was born. My earliest childhood memories were the best memories of my entire life. I felt safe, secure, and very much loved. My dad was a pastor of a church in Barstow, California. He was a caring father and he spent a lot of quality time with my sister and me. My mother was a good house wife who cooked us breakfast, lunch and dinner every day. She kept the house clean and kept the house together while my father would go to work to provide for our family. My dad made sure all of the bills were paid and none of us worried about anything. We lived in a nice home with expensive furniture and décor. We had a nice car as well. You could easily say we were living the American Dream. My father wanted us to have the best things in life so he worked his tail off to make sure we had the best. My mother, my sister, and I all looked up to him. We were a happy family. I remember the vacations we used to go on all the time. We would go camping and sometimes we would even go fishing. I did so many things with my dad that were so precious. He was the one person I thought could do no wrong. He used to help my sister and me out with our homework when we needed help. I remember he used to get mad and yell at me when I did not catch on to my school work as fast as he thought I should. This would make me cry and sometimes he would spank me for crying. He did none of this to be cruel even though I thought it was at that time. Now I understand his purpose was that he wanted my sister and me to be smart educated girls. My dad had my best interest at heart. He loved my sister and me. We were his girls and he wanted the best for us and yes he did discipline us when we needed discipline. Sometimes when my sister and I would get into trouble my mom would want to spank us and my father would ask us "Which one do you want to whoop you, your mother or me"? We would choose my dad. Then he would take us in the bedroom and shut the door. He would hit the bed and say to us "You all act like you are crying so your mother will think I am whooping you". Oh but when he spanked us for real, wow did it hurt. Of course he meant it for our good. He was trying to prepare us for the rough road of life. He would spoil my sister and me with so many toys. We had dolls and tea sets and bikes and games. It was like I had a fairy tale life. My dad even bought me a pony. Yes a pony. I was able to have a pony because we lived on a ranch. We had farm animals on the ranch like chickens and cows and pigs so a pony was just icing on the cake. My dad would not let me ride my pony unless he was right there with me. He used to put me on the pony and walk me around in a circle. I used to want to ride by myself but I guess dad did not trust the pony. On the ranch I used to feed our farm animals. We had a baby goat and I remember I used to feed him with a bottle. I fed our pigs slop. I used to enjoy life with both of my parents.

I also remember my parents ran a boy's home for troubled young men. You see, my parents had good hearts with good intentions that is why I never could have imagined that our lives would be completely turned upside down by them. Have you ever heard the old saying, "It will never happen to me", well that is not true. Anything can happen to anybody you just never know when. I don't quite remember when my parents started backsliding because I was too young to really know what was going on. I just know that was the worst thing that could have happened to our family. From that point on things got worse and worse. First my father started drinking. I guess he had a lot of pressure on him. I remember several occasions he drove around in the car while intoxicated with my sister and me in the back seat. We had no idea that our lives were in danger. My sister and I thought we were in good hands because we were with our dad. It's something how children are so trusting. They depend on their parents for safety, shelter, love, food, and other securities. It's also something how parents are often the ones who rob their own children of the things they depend on. In my case I was robbed of a lot of things by my parents and so was my sister. I never would have sleep overs at my house with my friends because I was too ashamed. I was ashamed of my addict parents and our living conditions. When I was younger I am sure I had fabulous birthday parties, but I don't ever remember having any as I grew older. My mom never taught me how to clean the house or cook a meal. She used to keep our house so clean when I was a small child but as time progressed she did less and less of her motherly duties. Most children have parents to teach and guide them. I had to figure out life of my own.

After my father started drinking, he then upgraded and began to smoke weed too. Then my mother started smoking weed along with him. When I was younger I did not think that weed and drinking was so bad. It was something I had been exposed to and I had learned to adapt to it. I thought everything my parents did was what parents were supposed to do. As a very small child I never felt worried or troubled. We had all the necessities of life. If we were struggling I didn't know it because I was happy and secure. But as time progressed my parents started to get high more and more often. I started to see things change and I didn't like what I was seeing. My parent's addiction cost us more than we bargained for.

When crack came into the picture it seems like it took over everything. Our family hit an all-time low. My father who was once a respected pastor and youth mentor began to look like a bum. I remember how embarrassing that was for me. When he would come to my school to pick me up I would feel so ashamed because he looked a mess. My mom always looked a mess too, but she would try to dress her mess up. She would have on tight pants and short, short dresses. She wore high heels and lots of make-up but her crack addiction made her look like walking death. People would always brag on the way she would dress because even though she was on crack she still tried to look decent. I really didn't care one way or the other how my parents dressed, I just wanted them delivered and off crack. We had everything before and I wanted things to be that way again. I thought the day would never come that my parents would get clean. As a child I think I accepted the lie that my parents would never be delivered.

My mom was strung out on crack for nineteen years. I always thought she would die a crack head. I even used to pray as a child that God would just take her out while she was going through one of her saved phases. You see my mom would call herself saved and delivered from crack every so often. I always knew, however, that she was never sincere. I knew that her so called salvation was only a temporary feeling that was in her head and not a permanent change that was in her heart. Sometimes these phases would last a day or two, or a week or so, or sometimes even a couple of months, but I always expected her to fall right back into the hands of crack. Whatever it was, it would override the fact that she could lose custody of my sister and me. What got me most was I didn't understand how crack was so powerful that it could make my mother neglect and misuse the ones she was willing to die for. Crack made her spend money that we needed for our rent and food. The needs we had made no difference to my mother. If she wanted crack she got it. It did not matter to her where the money came from or what we had to do without. The only thing that mattered to her was to get high. Crack was my mother's number one priority in life. I can remember one night my sister and I had not eaten dinner and my mom told us to go to bed. I guess she figured if we went to sleep we would not think about being hungry. She told us if someone came by with some money that she would wake us up to go get something to eat. We were fortunate that night that her boyfriend came by. I will never forget that night because he came into the house with some hamburgers, fries, and drinks. My mom woke us up and we were so happy to get that food. I sometimes wonder if she did that for us out of love or out of guilt because we were helpless and depended on her for everything. My mom chose to smoke crack all day everyday instead of making sure our needs were met. My sister and I were blessed in a sense because we never went without food or shelter. The food we had was not always what we wanted but we never starved. Even if we only got potatoes all day long we still got full. It seems like we always had a bag of potatoes at the house if we didn't have anything, regardless of the meal we always got full. As I look back on those times all I can say is God was watching over us.

As the years went by and I grew older my mother started selling crack as well as smoking it. During those days my sister and I always kept money in our pockets. My mother used to give me her drug money to hold for her. I used to sneak in her money and keep some of it for myself. My mom did not give me chump change either like fifty or sixty dollars no she gave me thousands of dollars at a time. My sister and I had rings on every finger and our nails done. We had money to buy expensive athletic shoes and designer clothes. We had all the things money could buy but we did not have our mother. I would have traded all those material things in a second to have my mother back. I wanted her back the way she was before when she was the preacher's wife. No matter how much I wished for my mom to change wishing was not enough. Crack had her and all the friends that she smoked crack with bound.

I used to ditch school with my friends almost every day. School was not important to me then because I did not realize the value of an education. It started out with just a few of us ditching school and just hanging out but before long there were about five or six of us doing it on a regular basis. Our favorite place to hang out when we ditched school would be the cemetery. Yeah that's right, the cemetery. I am sure you are thinking, "What a strange place to hang out". It was rather strange. Maybe us being there was like a metaphor or something. Our hope for our future was dead so we hung out with the dead. We went there because we knew no one would look for us in a cemetery. No truant officer would bother us there. I had peace of mind in the cemetery. It was quiet and clean. There were no addicts, no drug dealers, and no police were there either. The cemetery was our happy place. Most of the times we were there we would just sit around laughing and goofing off. Sometimes we would walk around the cemetery and read the names and dates on the tomb stones. We felt sorry for the ones who had died so young. How ironic it was for us that the place where most people found to be so sad and full of tears was the place where we found the most laughter and joy.

One time my sister and I ditched school with some of our friends and we were chased by the police. We were hanging out that day doing basically nothing when all of a sudden the police showed up. It caught us by surprise so we all ran in different directions. We knew that if everybody scattered and ran in different directions it would be hard for the police to catch us. We would laugh at them because it was a game to us. It was a game that is until one of us got caught. And that day the one that got caught was my little sister of all people. When I saw the officer grab her I knew it was serious. She was taken to jail and my mom was notified. I knew we were going to be in a lot of trouble then. Even though my mom was a crack addict, when we did something really bad she would discipline us. My sister had to stay in jail all day because the detention center would not release her to my mom right away. They wanted to teach her a lesson. Finally, after spending a whole day in jail my sister was released from holding. I still do not know how she was caught by the police. My mom was quite upset over the whole incident. She was mad at the police for keeping my sister so long and she was mad at us because we had no business skipping school. I am pretty sure the whole thing was embarrassing to my mom but that did not stop her from continuing to smoke crack.

My sister and I could leave home anytime we wanted to without asking permission. My mom didn't keep tabs on us she was too busy getting high. When my children were small if they had left the house without telling me they knew that was an automatic beat down. My mom on the other hand wasn't at home to ask permission for anything and if she was at home she did not want to be bothered with us. The only time she bothered to do anything to us or with us was if it interrupted her. You see my mom hardly took an interest in anything we did but if we got in trouble and she had to be informed we knew she was going to beat us. It was like out of sight out of mind. As long she didn't know what we were doing it was all good but if she had to take time out from her crack schedule we knew it was all over with. My mom wasn't always like that. When she and my dad pastored their church we had a respectable family. My mom and dad were home and they paid attention to us. How could things change so drastically? Those were the good times. Those were the crack free years.

II

The Separation

DRUGS BROUGHT ABOUT lots of changes that my family would have never expected. I think it may have even led to the separation of my mom and dad. After my mom and dad separated my sister and I wound up staying with my mother. I don't know how my parents became addicts I just know they were trapped in the wilderness of drugs and alcohol. They went from the pulpit to the crack house. As far as I can remember, I was about six or seven when all the drugs and alcohol started. My father wanted a way out so he decided to go to the army. I guess he thought that the army was his savior but it wasn't. Every time he came home to visit he would smoke crack right along with my mom. I used to call my dad an independent crack head. That means he always had a job and didn't have to hustle on the streets. Even though crack was his number one priority he still always provided for us. I can remember a time when my dad was home visiting and my mother had smoked some crack in front of me and my sister for the first time. Well the first time turned out to be the last time. Mr. Crawford (that's what I always called my dad when he began to smoke crack) beat my mom right in front of us for the first time. They both had a first time that day. My sister and I were so afraid we began to scream and cry. We were only helpless children and we did not fully understand what was going on.

As the years went by crack was always right there. Finally my mom and dad got divorced but neither one of them divorced crack cocaine. My dad never remarried. He stayed in the army and spent most of his time away with his army duties. I often wonder how he remained in the army for so long with his addiction. How is it that he never got kicked out? I believe that he only smoked crack when he came home to visit, but I could be wrong. I will say that was still amazing to me that he never was kicked out of the service. Anyway, when I was sixteen and my sister was fourteen my father was given a choice to reenlist or be discharged from the army. He gave my sister and me a choice too. He told us we could go to Germany where he would be stationed if he stayed in the army or we would move to Arkansas where his side of the family was living. Well, my sister and I chose Arkansas. We chose Arkansas because it was closer to California than Germany. You see my sister and I really, really loved California. We used to talk about how we never wanted to move from Cali and how we would make it our permanent home. We had our friends and our family there and I guess California was just a comfort to us. Germany was totally out of the question. It was so far away and we didn't know anyone there. We knew how to survive in California. So since Arkansas was closer than Germany we figured it would be easier to get back to California from Arkansas when we grew up than Germany. So that is how we wound up in Arkansas. My dad moved there first then he sent for us to come.

When I moved to Arkansas my school transcript was terrible. I had failing grades and incompletes in almost every class. I was always ditching school and my parents did not have any control over my behavior. I blamed them for my grades. Someone may not agree but I say that because if crack would not have had all of their attention they could have paid attention to me, my grades, and my school attendance. They could have helped me with school and cared like parents were supposed to but they had other issues. My dad stepped in right on time when he moved us to Arkansas. I was scared to ditch there because I had heard that your parents would go to jail for their children not attending in the state of Arkansas. I didn't want that to happen so I went to school and my sister did too. My senior year I made co-captain of the cheerleading squad but I had to drop cheerleading because I needed seven classes to graduate. That was disappointing to me but I did what I had to do. I worked hard and I turned all my failing grades into passing ones and graduated with my correct class in 1992.

After my father moved us to Arkansas my mom soon came to join us. She came with her crack. While we were in Arkansas my sister and I changed to a better way but my parents kept on smoking crack. We all lived together with my grandparents who did not seem to be too fond of us especially my sister and me. Sometimes they would treat us bad. These grandparents were my father's parents. His mother did not really care for my mother at all so therefore she did not rally care for my sister and me either. My grandmother showed favoritism toward her different sets of grandchildren. My sister and I were at the bottom of her list. My parents knew that our grandmother did not treat us right but crack ¹e them only see what they wanted to see. They felt as long as we

KAREY RUSSELL & EVANGELIST MYRA PRATT

were provided a place to sleep at night and had food to eat we were okay. Crack did not allow them to see that we were dogged out all the time. I remember my grandmother used to get all of the grandchildren presents for Christmas except my sister and me. She would tell us that she would get us something later and say that she did not forget about us. Of course later never came, we never saw our gifts. She used to say things like "I can't stand you. You look just like your mama". I guess my grandmother's anger and resentment for my mom clouded her judgment. Maybe she was hurting inside too because it's been said that hurting people hurt other people. Whatever the cause for her behavior it was very hurtful for my sister and me. Later in my life when my sister and I had children my mom turned around and showed favoritism to them. So my sister and I were still on the bottom of the list. My mom and dad never put us first they always cared more about crack and getting high. Both my sister and I basically had to do things on our own. If we were to be successful that it was up to us. God was truly with us because we both managed to graduate from high school. I did not go to college. I had two sons and later became God mother of two little girls. Somehow I have always been blessed with decent paying jobs that put me in the middle class status. My sister did go to college. She is now a registered nurse. She is married with four beautiful children. I thank God that we did not turn out the way our parents did and I can now thank God for crack free parents. They started off crack grandparents but I'm not quite sure if any of the grandchildren can actually remember those days. As for me, I wish those days had never happened and I sure do wish I could forget them. At least now I can say that those days are over and gone. Thank God.

III

Life with Addicts

MY PARENTS STARTED off being crack head grandparents but they made a change for the better. They may have been pitiful parents too but they are now doing well as grandparents. Before my parents got clean I could tell some stories about them. I remember this one time I had left my kids at home with my mom at five in the morning. At that time my boys were very young; one of them was four the other one was seven. I had to be at work at 5:45 a.m. After I had left them a bad feeling about leaving them came over me by the time I got to work. Something told me to call home so I did. When I called I did not get an answer. I called again and again but my mom did not answer the phone. Later I found out that my mom had left my four year old and seven year old at home all by themselves. I was so angry. I thought to myself "What if the house caught on fire or somebody had broken in"? When I got to my mom I fussed at her like crazy. I always used to fuss at her when she was an addict. It seemed like everything that went on in those days led to me fussing at her. One time I had a piggy bank that I was keeping all my spare change in for my children. I had accumulated quite a bit of change too. Well my mom stole all the money that I had been saving for my kids. Even though it was nothing but a lot of change I was still very upset because how could she do that to her own grandchildren and me? She made me so furious that I wanted to fight her. I called her all kinds of four letter words in my mind. I wanted to say it to her but I was taught at a young age to respect my elders. But now that I think about it I probably would have called her a choice word right to her face if she would have been there at that moment. The amount of money she took was not the issue. I was just so hurt that my mom was now so addicted and out of control that she would steal from her own grandbabies.

One time I was at home asleep on the couch. I kept my rent money in my pillow case in my bedroom. All of a sudden my mother woke me up she said "Karey your baby, look at the baby he's got your money". I took the money my son had and counted it and some of the money was missing. No one seemed to know where the missing money was especially my mom. I blamed her for stealing it because she was on crack. Right to this day she says she didn't get that money. Another incident that happened led up to me putting my mom out of my house. I had some jewelry in my bedroom and it came up missing and just like with the missing rent money no one knew what had happened to it. I later had to apologize because the jewelry had popped back up after my mom left. I don't know if she put it back or if she had someone else to put it back, all I know is I had it back after I put her out. Later on after my mom was drug free, I asked my mom did she do any of the things I accused her of doing while she was on crack. She told me that she would rather me not ask her questions because then she would have to tell the truth. We both laughed. It's good to be able to look back and laugh now. I know I am not the only one who accused my mom of doing some under handed things that she probably did not do. But crack makes you guilty automatically of everything. My father did things that made no sense just like my mother. I remember this one time he asked me if he could borrow my car. I guess I thought I could trust him so I gave him my keys. I didn't even hesitate. After all this was my dad I was not expecting him to do anything but bring the car back when he finished with it. Well, I was totally shocked over what happened next. My father had the gall to go and sell my car to get him some crack. That's right some crack. The person he sold the car to must have been as Looney as he was because my dad didn't even have the title to the car. When I confronted my dad about the car he admitted to me that he had sold it so he could go get high. How you gone sell somebodies car after they let you borrow it? Maybe he thought I wouldn't notice it was missing? Are you serious? That's the kind of stuff that give crack heads a bad name.

 Crack makes people do some crazy things to the people they love. Anyway, I sure do thank God that both my parents are delivered today. It took many years and my mom going to prison for them to change. Oh yes, my mom went to prison for two years. I didn't feel sorry for her then but now that I work for a prison I know what it is like to be incarcerated. Sometimes I think that her time in prison helped her realize that she needed to change her lifestyle. I think she had a slap in the face by reality. My mom's incarceration helped her realize that she did not want to be an addict anymore. It was a life altering experience for her. When she got out I was amazed to see her with a new look and a new attitude. She was a new creature in Christ. This time though she wasn't just putting on an act. She had really been transformed. It took a year or two maybe for me to actually believe what I was seeing. It turned out after all those years mother was finally delivered! I am so thankful to God. I never thought I would see it after all the time that had passed us by. Sometimes I say to myself she should have gone to prison a long time ago, I'm joking of course. I am not saying that prison helps everyone because it doesn't. It was God who gave my mom the grace to be delivered and stay delivered. Without Him it would have been impossible. Addiction is a spirit and you can't fight a spiritual problem with physical weapons. 2Corinthians 10:4 says, "The weapons of our warfare are not carnal but mighty through God to the pulling down of strongholds". My mom went through rehab, and hospital stays, and counseling yet she always came home a bigger crack addict than she was before. Addiction is a spiritual battle that you will lose every time without a higher power. Ephesians 6:12 says, "For we wrestle not against flesh and blood but against principalities, against powers, against the rulers of the darkness of this world, against spiritual wickedness in high places". I heard people talk about a higher power. I am glad in my mom's case God was and is her higher power. Believe it or not He is the only higher power that can keep us delivered. I thank God for the sacrifice of Jesus because without his blood my mom would have no hope. There is no addiction that can intimidate God and there is no circumstance that is too big for Him to handle. God is still in the miracle working business. I say that because if His power delivered my mom then His power can deliver anyone. My mom was one of the worst types of addicts that you ever wanted to see. Not because of the way she looked but because of the way she was. She definitely lived by "whatever you hand finds to do, do it with all of your might" because she did the crack game with all her might. I mean one-hundred percent. She was a fast talker and she could basically talk her way out of anything. She could hustle the best hustler and play the best player. She could steal something you owned right from under your nose and then turn around a sell it back to you. When she was around you had to watch your back because she would rob you or set you up to get robbed. She used to pimp men and women and use them to get her next high. That is why I know it was God who stepped in on my mom's behalf. God is no respecter of persons (Acts 10-34) He is Love and He loved my mom even when she did not know how to love herself or her children.

When my parents first split up my sister and I lived with our mom. Our house was like the neighborhood hangout house. My mother always had strange people in our house. There were men and women, young and old, and they would be there day and night. My mom had a stream of constant traffic back and forth from her bedroom especially at night. Her bedroom was where everyone went to smoke crack. I guess my mom thought my sister and I didn't know what was going on in there. She would send us to our room to go to bed at night like everything was peaches and cream. We weren't stupid. We knew all those people were there for crack. I hardly ever got any sleep. How could I sleep? It was always noisy. Sometimes I tried to sleep through the noise but I couldn't because they would be so loud it sounded like they were in my room with me. I could hear the crack heads arguing over who would take the next hit. They would laugh one minute and then cuss each other out the next. I could hear it all and I do mean "all" that went on in that bedroom and none of it was good. I remember how scared I was all the time. I did not know who those strange people in my house were and I didn't know what they would do to me. When they would come out of my mom's bedroom high I could see their big, bubble, bulging eyes. They would look like crazy people and they acted that way too. They stank because they smelled like crack. They looked like they were paranoid and scared. If I would have said boo to one of them they probably would have jumped out of their skin. I stayed away from them as much as I could because I did not like any of them. I did not like my mother either. I loved her because she was mom but I hated that she was a crack addict. I also hated that she preferred her crack buddies over me and my sister. I didn't trust any of those addicts and I did not trust my mother either. I wanted my old mommy back but I couldn't have her. She belonged to crack and not me.

Most of the memories I have about my parents are sad memories I did not want to be like them at all. They really had no idea what I was going through as a child. Children should be able to depend on their parents to prepare them for the things this world has to offer so when they grow up they will know how to function in life. Children should not be put in harm's way. Children should not be neglected. Children should feel loved. I was robbed of all those things. We had a good family once upon a time but crack changed my good parent into dead beats who cared only about themselves.

My parents would sell their possessions and government benefits for drugs and alcohol. They didn't think about their obligation to my sister and me. They just wanted to get a crack thrill. Crack made them selfish and uncaring. Sometimes addicts lose all compassion for their children. Some children have been beaten or even killed by their own parents. Crack can make a person hallucinate and act down right foolish. I thank God that He protected my sister and me from that kind of abuse. I shudder every time I think about someone doing such horrible things to their own children. Some addict parents have allowed drug dealer to rape and molest their children just so they can get high. I'm not talking about teenagers, no I mean little children that are no more than nine or ten years old. Some addicts have taken the side of drug dealers against their own children and they will not believe their children when they try to tell them what their offenders have done to them. I couldn't imagine my child coming to me and me taking someone else's side against them. I am like an angry lion when it comes to my children. If you touch them I will tear you apart. I am like that because I know what it is like for children who have been victimized. I know what it is like to feel afraid and scared to tell on the person who violated you. I know this because I was molested by my uncle when I was very young.

One night when my parents were out on one of their crack binges, my sister and I had to stay over my aunt's house. I was about seven or eight years old at that time. We were there for a while at auntie's house doing what we usually do when my aunt said she had to step out for a minute. She had to go somewhere in a hurry so she left us at home alone with her husband. She told us we could go to bed and if we needed anything our uncle was there to watch us. I remember I was about to go to bed and I wanted a glass of water before I went to sleep. I went to my uncle and asked him if he could pour me a glass of water. He was more than eager to get it up and get it for me. He looked around to see if anyone else was with me then he told me to come into the kitchen. I was just a trusting innocent child so I had no idea a man could be sexually attracted to a little girl. I wasn't taught about touching or inappropriate behavior. I did not have "the talk" with my mom or dad. My mom's advice about sex education was "don't give it away for free".

My uncle poured me a glass of water then he gave it to me. As I started to drink it he put his hands on my behind. He began to rub on me and caress my bottom like I was his lover. He pulled me to him and looked at me in a way I had never seen him look at me before. It was so creepy. I felt very uncomfortable but this was my uncle so why would he hurt me? My uncle kept touching me then he said, "Baby girl you gone be so fine when you grow up cause you got a nice body already".

He said, "With the body you got you gone be a fox". That's old school slang meaning an attractive woman with a big behind. I stood there all confused. I did not know what to do or say. It is so frightening for a child to be placed in a situation where they have to make grown up decisions. It is so unfair for adults to put them in that predicament. I did not know about relationships between a man and a woman, but I knew what my uncle was doing to me wasn't right. I was just a kid and I could not defend myself against this man. I was trembling inside and I was trying to hold back my tears to be strong. I guess my uncle could see I was afraid because he looked at me with a somewhat caring expression and said, "This will be our little secret okay Karey"? Then he said with a whisper, "Don't tell anybody about this okay"? I didn't respond to him I just tried to get as far away from him as I could. I get disgusted every time I think about what could have taken place. He could have raped me and no one would have ever known. My parents were addicts and I don't think they were even capable at that time to be there for me and my sister. My parents had no idea what anyone was saying to me or doing to us. Did they care where we were or what we were doing? I don't know. I just know they were not there to protect me.

    I remember after my uncle fondled me I was too ashamed to tell my parents or anyone else about what he had done. I was ashamed even though I had not done anything wrong. I had to go through all that hurt and embarrassment alone. My daddy wasn't there to dry my tears or defend me. I was afraid. Not because my uncle threaten me but because I felt danger. Who could I turn to for help when I was in danger? I know if my parents were not addicts they would have never let me stay at my aunt and uncle's house because my parents knew my uncle was an alcoholic and a drug addict. I know many people who have had worse experiences than me but regardless of that I know if children are not protected there are sick minded people who will take advantage of them. As a child of addict parents I have known about many sick minded people. I still to this day, don't see why any grown man would want to have sex with a little girl. I can't understand that type of sick mindset. I can't understand inflicting that type of mental and physical abuse on a child. I wish I could wrap my arms around every victim of abuse and give them the comfort and healing they need. God helped me by protecting me and giving me the ability to forgive. I do not hold grudges against my parent because I know they were sick. They had a terminal illness called "crack cocaine".

I can't change what happened to me and I can't punish my uncle or my parents. I had to learn to let it go.

    I want to encourage every person who had parents with an addiction. You have the power to rise above your circumstance. We could all make bad choices and follow in our parent's footsteps or we can choose a different outcome for ourselves. Our parents whether we like it or not are our first role models. We see them as everything so when they let us down their failure has a greater weight to us than if it were someone else. I remember I used to wish I had the kind of parents that I saw on TV. It seemed like the Cosby's had it all together. They were the cool parents. I could only daydream about being in a family like that. In my dream we would have the big house and I would wear all the pretty clothes. I would have nice sports car. My mom would be the successful career woman who had it altogether. When she walked into a room everyone would stop and stare at her beauty. My dad would be the funny comedian that made you laugh all the time. He would be kind and he would always protect me. My daydreams however, turned into nightmares when I woke up. I say that because my big pretty house was anybody's house. My sister and I stayed with anyone and everyone who let us in. Whenever my mom walked into a room people did stare at her. Yes, she got a lot of stares because she looked like a walking skeleton. She was like I said before a dressed up mess. A hot mess! No one would have been able to convince her that she wasn't cute. Most addicts look horrible but in their minds they think they still got it. They could have teeth missing, no hair, and smell like death but you can't tell them nothing. As for my dad he made you laugh alright. You'd laugh when you saw him because he looked like a bum. He was a drunk and a crack head. That combination just screams comedian. If we would have had a reality show ours' would have the number one rating. It would be "Meet the Crawfords, America's Favorite Dysfunctional Crack Family".

    I thought everybody had good parents except me. Now I know that my parents and all parents are humans who do make mistakes and I should not put my hope in them but in the Lord. I know God is everything I used to wish my parents were. He gave my parents what they needed to change. So now instead of wishing I had great parents I confess that I do have great parents. I try to see the positive in all of the negativity. I say if my parents would not have been such awful parents I would not know how to be a good parent. I think about everything that hurt me and I strive not to do it to my children. It hurts to be lonely and talked about by your family members. My parent's addiction helped me to see the importance of family and having a support base. It helped me to see the value of children and how precious and innocent they are. Their mistakes made me determined to get an education and make something better happen for me and my children. The neglect I endured and the abuse I saw my mother go through showed me that I never wanted to be in a bad marriage or abusive relationship. Every time I saw my mom get hit it was like someone hit me too. I worried about her and I did not want anything to bad to happen to her. I had to learn through the things I suffered to stay calm in every situation. Staying calm can keep you alive and out of prison.

My parent's addiction taught me that I did not have true love. Crack is a drug that the devil uses to destroy people. I know this because it is the opposite of love. Crack deceived my parents' minds and it made them very selfish. I am sure if someone would have asked my mom during her addiction if she were a good mom she would have told them yes because she thought she was doing the best for her children. My mom was only maintaining because she had an obligation. When she came off her high I'm sure she felt sorry about the way she was, but there was not enough love in her to give up crack for us. Love makes a person do right and make right choices. God is love. Love is what made me able to look over and forgive all those who wronged me and put me through struggle. Forgiving at times was all I had to hold on to. I had to look at Jesus and depend on Him because He was my inspiration and He never turned his back on me. My sister and I basically raised ourselves because my parents remained addicts for years. I used to think my parents would die as crack heads but they proved me wrong. Now they both have been delivered and have remained drug free and I give God all the glory for that.

Life is full of problems that's for sure, so I had to learn and an early age how to handle problems. Staying calm is what helped me to determine if I would be successful or not. Sometimes people like to stereo-type children of addicts. It is like they are waiting to see us fail and lose it. I think a lot of people would have been happy to see me go into a psychotic rage and hurt someone. I have heard people say "Oh she gone be just like her mama; a crack head". I could have done the same thing as someone else but I had to be labeled as a future addict just because my parents were addicts. Those types of words are so hurtful but I did not let them define me. God gave me the courage to get myself together. My sister and I were easily able to become addicts. We had every opportunity to get high. We had every opportunity to get locked up. And we also had every opportunity to get "dead". It was hard for my sister and me to make right choices because we did not have much parental guidance. It is not what people say we are or think we are that matters however. It's what we are and what we think we are that is going to make the difference in our lives. Proverbs 23:7 says, as a man thinks in his heart so is he. And Proverbs 18:21 says, life and death are in the power of the tongue. So in other words we are what we think of ourselves. We are what we say about ourselves. So I decided to think of myself in a positive way. I do not care if people do not see what is good about me. What I think is what matters. I am not the daughter of crack addicts. I am a successful young woman who made it out of a difficult past. I am not a failure. I just fell seven times and then got up. I am not poor nor am I a statistic. I am prosperous. I am not a victim. I am a mentor and I encourage others. I am somebody who motivates people to do what is right. I had to make up my mind to think this way and not let anyone else make my mind up for me.

Many people do not understand the psychological damage that addiction causes. I was placed in a situation where I had no hope. It was impossible for me to get out by myself, but I found out all things are possible with God. I had to make a decision. If you are under the care of addicts seek God for the answers to your problem don't look to yourselves. Proverbs 14:12 says, There is a way that seems right to a man but its end is the way of death. You can have a lot of anger and no one can blame you for feeling that way, but anger won't help it will only hinder your progress. I say that because when you find Christ you find love, peace, comfort, friendship and compassion. You learn that love draws people to you. Then those people will take you under their wings and pray for you and hope the best for you. Even if you fail love will let you know it's okay. No one can take your will to do what is right or wrong but you. When people can see an eagerness for success in you they respect it. They will stop all the negative speaking about how you will turn out and they will start speaking positive words about you. Like I said before what people think or say is not the most important thing that matters. There is a better life than the ones our parents offered. It is possible to have a better life if you choose it. Sometimes well-meaning people or I call them "religious people" will hurt your feelings. They may see you doing well but they are expecting you to fail. As long as you are doing the best you can to the best of your ability then you are actually better off than they are. Remember it is not those people who can help you out it is God. Stay encouraged and keep striving because your own choices will affect your life just as much as your parents will. It is not hard to choose right over wrong when you find Jesus. He is our guide and he is qualified to lead us and teach us. Get rooted and grounded in Him and be immovable and trust in Him. Depend on Him and He will be there for you. He will never turn His back on you or put a drug ahead of you. He will not let you down and he will not put you down. He will forgive you and help you to forgive others, especially those who have hurt you the most. I had to forgive my parents and my past. If I didn't it would have consumed me. I could worry over my parents and hold grudges until I was sick but it would not help them. It could not help them. My parents were addicts for nineteen years. Those years cost me a lot. My anger, my pain, and my frustration were real but I could not constantly dwell on it for my own sake. Unforgiveness is like a cancer that eats at you night and day. God says if I don't forgive others for the wrongs they have done then he will not forgive me for the wrongs I have done. (Mark 11:26) We all need God's forgiveness. In my opinion the worst person to hang around is a bitter unforgiving person who complains about everything everyone has done to them since 1846. Nobody wants to hear a person blame others for their failures. I made the decision to be a better person. People get weak to temptation and their own thoughts. Jesus was tempted as we are but he did not succumb to the temptation. (Hebrews 4:15) He was strong and He wants you to be strong. I was given a second chance to change. My parents were too. We have changed our behavior by the grace of God. God gives us the desire to change.

IV

The Desire to Change

I THANK GOD that He helped me to change. The same way God helped me He can help you so you won't head down the road of destruction. He will give you the power to do it. Of course the devil wants you to believe you are doomed to be a product of your environment. He wants to keep you bound and stuck where you are, but in case you did not know it the devil is a liar and there is no truth in him. (John 8:44) There is always a way with God to get back on track. I like that my mom used that phrase for the title of this book because that's what it is all about getting back on track.

My sister and I never really had a family life except for when I was very young. There was no movie night with popcorn and Kool-Aid. We didn't sit at the dinner table and tell how our day was. No one was there to check my homework after school or sign my report card to see if my grades were satisfactory. My sister and I did not have curfews. We hung out as long as we wanted. We could come in at eleven at night or five in the morning. I guess we were considered thugs. The sad part is no one cared that we were out. Where was our mom? Oh she was at the crack house with the neighborhood crack heads hosting the festivities. I remember one time my sister and I were living with a friend of mine. We had gone to her house to spend one night but we ended up staying there many nights. Finally my friend asked her mom if we could just live with them because we did not have any place to go. Her parents agreed to let us move in. I don't even know if my parents knew where we were. My friend's parents were not on crack or anything like that. They basically just worked all the time. They were always gone so we still were able to do whatever we wanted to do and my friend was right along with us. My sister and I began to hang out more and more and anyone in their right mind knows that unsupervised young people, especially teens can be your worst nightmare. We became delinquents. I am sure that was what a lot of people expected because like I said before people used to say "You gone wind up just like your mama, a crack head". I remember one night some of my friends and I got some eggs and egged some people's houses. That stuff stinks like crazy after a day or two. We didn't care everything was funny to us. Everything was a game. I wonder sometimes was it a desperate cry for someone to notice us. For someone to say "Hey you do matter and you are important" We had no consequences to face and that probably was the hurt that drove our delinquency. We played pranks on old people especially the tired old "ring the doorbell and run before they answered the door" routine. My friends and I used to go around and find empty wine cooler bottle. We would burst them against the wall outside of our neighborhood convenience store. I guess we wanted someone to cut their foot on the glass. We started out doing silly childhood pranks but as we got older we wanted bigger thrills so we went to the next level. I remember when we started drinking and getting drunk. Nothing was more exciting at that time in my life than to get some liquor. We were too young to buy liquor ourselves so we had to hustle ways to get it. We could always find an addict who was willing to help us. Any street smart hustler knows you can always get a crack head to get you anything you wanted if you gave them a few dollars to get a crack rock. A crack head will be your most loyal friend if they think you can help them get a rock. Sometimes we could get some of our friends' older siblings to buy us what we wanted but the biggest excitement we had over getting liquor was to go in the store and steal it. We knew just how to do it to because we had this system. One person would create a diversion like breaking something on the floor, or causing a scene. The other person kept a look out and someone else stole the liquor. We were professionals. Yeah it was funny to us to. It was the ultimate victory to get away with a crime. I was so naïve and too stupid to know that a drunk young woman on the streets at night is every lowlife's fantasy. I am surprised no one took advantage of me or my sister. I jokingly say "The angels had to work over time for us" because we were never harmed. I know there were people praying for us.

    I hated the addiction my parents had but that did not deter me from smoking weed. I started smoking weed about the same time I started drinking. I was very young. It was easy for me to start smoking weed because most of the people I hung out with sold weed. There were some lucrative weed businesses in my part of town. If you couldn't get a job you could always start your own business selling weed. I did not think smoking weed was so bad because after all it wasn't crack. I reasoned like everyone else who wants to justify smoking it. You know the line, "Weed comes from the earth. Weed is just an herb". Most of the people who say that are holding a joint in their hand and exhaling smoke in your face wasting time and doing nothing. My parents did not know I was smoking weed. If they did they probably would have wanted some of my weed to smoke. Weed can consume your life just like crack. To me, liquor and weed are like the stepping stones to heavier drugs. Why would I even attempt to smoke weed if I hated my parents crack? I fought my whole life not to be like them and it seemed like I was more like them than I wanted to admit.

I began to experiment with sex a very young age just like with everything else. I think I was about twelve years old the first time I had sex. Can you imagine your twelve year old sexually active, especially your daughter. I am not saying it would be okay for a boy. Any parent in their right mind would not want this for their child male or female. My parents were too strung out to know what my sister and I were doing. I could have gotten pregnant or contracted an STD because I did not use protection. My mom did not have time to educate me about sex because she was too busy out in the streets having more sex than I was. She had to do what she had to do to support her crack habit. My sister and I didn't think we were doing anything wrong even though we knew better. That probably does not make sense to most. We knew our parents did not want us out being promiscuous but we figured we weren't hurting anybody. That is hard for someone who has never been in that situation to understand. We thought we were happy and that we were having fun but we were wrong. We were the girls that other parents did not want their children to hang around. We were what everyone expected us to be. I thank God for my grandmother on my mom's side, my aunts, uncles, and some of my friend's parents because they are the ones who kept us out of the foster care system.

I began to socialize with gang bangers about the same time I started drinking, smoking and having sex. I had a lot of friends who were in gangs. I remember the alley where we all used to hang out. That was our spot. We had some good times together. The gang members were more family to me than my parents were. One time we were in the alley just chillin when all of a sudden out of nowhere this car rolled up and someone started shooting at us. You should have seen us. We all scattered like ants. We were ducking and dodging the bullets and laughing all at the same time. We did not even have enough sense to realize how much danger we were in. I think we even got a rush out of it. That was what was expected in the gang world. No one ever knew if they would make it to the next day, or week, or year. We just lived life in the moment. One of the gang bangers that I hung around with eventually became my boyfriend. He was tough and he protected me. I was never officially a member of a gang because in order for a female to become a member they would have to have sex with one of the members of the gang as an initiation rite. My sister however, did become a member. I was considered a member because my boyfriend was one. Anyway, no one cared that my sister and I were "claiming sets". That was the street lingo for gang banging back then. My mom certainly did not care because my boyfriend was the dope dealer that sold her her crack. He sold crack to his own mother as well. His mom and my mom were on the same level, crack heads. Many people would not understand anyone selling crack to their own mother, but my boyfriend and me knew that they were addict. They were going to buy crack from somebody no matter what, so it may as well be him. We just kept it in the family. That was normal to us in the world we lived in. Did I care that my mom was buying crack from him? Not really. Crack was the only thing that my mom was interested in and I knew that if she dealt with him she was safe. Many times drug deals can go wrong especially if you are buying from someone you don't know. I didn't want my mom to buy from an undercover cop then wind up in jail. I didn't want her to get a hold of any bad drugs and lose her mind. Neither did I want my mom to die. Life on the street was dangerous. I loved my mom even though she did not know how to love me the way I needed to be loved.

It is a miracle I did not wind up in jail because my parents may not have cared about what I did but the L.A.P.D. did care. They cared not out of love; they just wanted to keep the community safe from gang bangers and hoodlums like me and my friends. They wanted to protect society from us. But who was protecting us? The streets I guess. We turned to the streets of Compton and L.A. when we could not turn to our parents. My boyfriend eventually wound up in prison. He was in and out a couple of times. Those trips eventually led him to stop gang banging. He made a choice like I did and now he is a totally different person. His sister and I were best friends. We both knew the pain that crack could inflict on a person's life. Her friendship was dear to me because I could talk to her and she knew exactly what I was going through. We both had the same circumstance but not the same outcome. She ended up a crack addict in the end. She didn't get out. Now she is locked up in prison and her children were taken from her. I found myself at one time, after I was grown, wanting to sell drugs. I had one child at that time and it was hard being a single mom. I knew how much money a person could make by selling drugs because I had seen it all my life. If I had followed through with that temptation I could have possibly wound up in jail and had my children taken from me. Some of my other friends that I grew up with are dead now. Some are locked up and some are addicts like our parents were. It makes me sad to think about us all growing up the way we did. It makes me even sadder to know that for every one of us there was, there are hundreds more going through the same thing now.

My mother never knew about all the things I did as a teen until this book was written. She told me "I ought to spank you and your sister's butt for being juvenile delinquents". We both laughed. My mom said now that she is sober she feels so sorry for neglecting us. She knows that we forgive her and she knows God does too. God was there when we thought no one cared.

V

The True Way

GOD WILL BE with you whenever you need you Him and He will watch over you when you do not even expect Him to. What I mean by that is when you do not understand or do not see a way he will make a way. And times when things could go wrong He steps in and makes them right. I thank God that he had another plan for my life. My plan was not the vision God had for me. By His grace I am glad I had the sense to choose another road for my life. You see, I understand that God knows everything about us and where we will end up, but he still gives us opportunity to choose. Even though He already knows our choice and consequences or reward He allows us to choose. He wants everyone to make the right choice but He already knows what we will do before we do it. We can pretend to be something we are not for a while, but we cannot trick God. People can have as many opinions about you as they want but the only opinion you need to trust is God's. What God says is the truth. So I choose to say what he says. God's spirit, the Holy Spirit will lead no one astray. The way out for me was available for me all along but I did not know it because I was not in the word. I did not know the word. The word of God is what produces the change. The word gives us the mind to change. It doesn't matter how bad you start the important thing is how you end up.

Do you find yourself trying to please others or do you find yourself outside of the box so you can be a light to the people of the world? Do you see yourself as a failure or a success? Well if you are saved you are a success no matter what has happened to you or what you have done. If you want to be a help to other people and lead them to salvation then you must first have it for yourself. It is easy to find and it is easy to keep. Roman 10:9 says if you confess with your mouth the Lord Jesus and shall believe in your heart that God has raised him from the dead, you shall be saved. For with the heart man believes unto righteousness; and with the mouth confession is made unto salvation. After you have done this yourself then you can be an awesome leader who can lead others to the right higher power, Jesus. That is what my mom and dad finally did. I could not get my father to share much of anything about his life as an addict but my mom was more than willing. She felt if her story could be told for the right reason, which is to help someone, then she would be doing what God wants her to do. That is to testify. So here is my mom's story of how she got Off Crack and Back on Track.

I

Introduction to Crack

I REALLY HOPE and I believe that this book will open the eyes of anyone who is an addict and give them revelation. I also intend for this book to deter non-crack smokers from becoming smokers. I will start at the beginning of my addiction. You see I was introduced to crack by someone over twenty years ago and that someone was me. I started out the typical way of selling crack as a drug dealer. And just like the statistics show I wound up using my own product and became by best customer. When I sold drugs to addicts I would watch them get high. I would look at their facial expressions and I would watch how they acted. They would look like they were in another world. They went to a place that I can't describe with words. Watching them made me feel like I was missing out on something. I wanted to know what they felt. I wanted that kind of pleasure that "ecstasy". I was foolish enough to think I could try something like crack one time and not get hooked. One of the biggest lies the devil will tell you is "Oh, it won't happen to me". I wonder how many people in the world have gotten infected with STD's, or pregnant, or raped, or even killed from that deceptive thought. I didn't know that the devil had a trap for me that would consume my whole life. I becamemore and more curious about getting high every time I watched someone smoke crack. I had never used crack before in my life but it had an allure that was almost mesmerizing. I don't even think I was scared at all when I tried it because I had gotten comfortable around it. The scripture says in I Corinthians 15:33, evil communication corrupts good manners. In other words whatever you are exposed to long enough will have an effect on you. If you associate with drugs, or sex, or homosexuality it's just a matter of time before it becomes normal to you. I remember I took that first hit and WOW it took me on a roller coaster ride! I can't lie to you because I want to keep this testimony real. Neither do I want to glamorize crack but that crack high took me to a state of pure euphoria. It took me to what I thought was the "Promised Land". It made me want to feel that pleasure over and over again. I was so into the high that the consequences of my actions never fazed me. As time progressed however I realized what a big mistake I had made. It wasn't long until crack wasn't fun anymore. It became a burden and I realized I was hooked. I had to constantly spend all my money that I was making selling drugs on drugs for myself. I also tried desperately to get that same feeling that I got the first time I took that hit but I never could. See no one tells you that crack is a deceiver. It is a lying spirit that keeps one chasing after it like a dog chasing its own tail. You never get that feeling again that you get from that first hit. No never. So there I was hooked on crack and for what, a good time? Trying to be like everyone else? I began to stay in the streets day and night. I stole, I cheated, and I lied to get to my next high. Crack had me standing on corners selling my body. I would get in and out of cars with different men. I didn't know if they were dangerous or not but if they had a dollar that would be their lucky day. I had guns put to my head on several occasions. I was thrown out of moving cars because of deals gone badly. I even did time in prison indirectly for chasing a crack rock. Sometimes when I was broke and craving a hit I would think to myself "I should have stuck with weed and never tried that crack." I know it's not good to be bound by any addiction or any drug. Weed will deteriorate your life and your health just like crack. I knew this man who smoked weed until he became incoherent. The only reason I would have wanted to smoke weed more than crack was because weed was less expensive. On several occasions I went to different rehabilitation center to get help. Needless to say I always came out more of an addict than when I went in. I was a train wreck and I felt I had no way out. I knew I needed help because my habit was expensive and it was taking its toll on me. The rehab centers were unsuccessful in helping me. Crack addition is spiritual and spiritual problems require spiritual solutions. I thank God that I am not in bondage to any drug anymore. My body is the temple of the Most High God and I refuse to live any old kind of way.

 Crack cocaine addiction is also a disease. It is just like cancer. It will eat at a person until they look like a walking corpse. So many of my good friends have died crack related deaths. Crack is the work of the devil. I know this for a fact because John 10:10 says "The thief (the devil) comes only to kill, steal, and destroy". Crack addiction does that exact thing. It will steal your entire life away before you even realize it. I have seen addicts in their twenties who have lost their teeth and look aged and tired. Crack will destroy everything you have and everything you are. Then it will eventually kill you. I am fortunate that my life was spared by God

Almighty who delivered me before the devil could kill me with crack. I tell in this book my account of the devastation of a life of crack. This is a true testimony and no matter how much havoc crack cocaine caused in my life God was bigger than crack. That is why today I can honestly say I am now off crack and back on track.

II

I did it For Crack

I DID THINGS as an addict that I would not dare think of doing now that I am sober and clean. I used to have some friends that I liked to smoke with on a regular basis. I liked to get high and if there was an opportunity for me to smoke I was going to take it. We used to go to hotel rooms and rent sex toys (these were electronic sexual devices we used as a substitute for a man). Sometimes when we were high all of us would sleep in the same bed. There we would fondle each other and we would also use the sex toys on each other. I thought it was all fun and games like a dare or something. I just wanted to add some fun to getting high but little did I know I was inviting lesbian spirits into my life. One of the friends I used to fool around with began to like me a romantic way. I remember the first time I met her. She was walking the streets late at night looking for crack. She looked so sad and troubled that I felt sorry for her. I wanted to encourage her because I have always been good at encouraging people. Years ago when my first husband and I had our own church I encouraged people all the time so I guess some of that was still in me, but I will talk about that later. Anyway that night I talked to this girl for a little while and I gave her a big hug to encourage her and let her know everything would be alright. Later I found out that one hug had triggered something in her and it would take years to get her out of my life. Let me stress this point to you; I am not a lesbian although I did participate in lesbian acts. I did do certain things that would make a person assume I was a lesbian but in my heart it was nothing I desired to be. When I started getting high I hooked up with this girl. She was really pretty I think she was Hispanic or something. We all would do goofy girl stuff while we were getting high. When you are an addict it really does not matter who you get high with or how you get high the important things is to GET HIGH. So if I had to rub a few butts and squeeze some breasts to get a hit, hey that is what I did. After a while I began to realize that this girl was serious about me. She wanted to hook up with me but I did not like her like that. I only did what I did to get high. I was not trying to get into a relationship. When I ignored her she began stalking me. She told my children "I'm in love with your mom." I told her countless times that I was not interested in her but the more I rejected her the more obsessed she became. Every man that I met and got involved with she slept with them to break us up. She even slept with one of my ex-husbands to keep him from me. She acted like she was going to stop at nothing to have me to herself. Sometimes when we were out getting high we would still get rooms together to turn our tricks to make money. This woman would actually pay my tricks not to sleep with me right in front of my face. She was determined to have me but I was determined not to wind up her woman. I remember there was this guy that I really liked and we were very much involved with each other. We moved in together and he bought me this nice car. It was an Audi and I loved that car. Well I cannot tell you how shocked and outraged I was this one day when I look up and saw this woman come over to my house driving my car, that I loved, that my man had bought for me. "Oh no you didn't", I thought to myself. "Why was this psycho driving my car"? She told me that she had given my man oral sex, and did some freaky sex acts with him to seduce him. She told me that she had blown his mind and that he was her man now so he let her have my car. (the car that I loved) When she told me that I didn't even bother to argue with her or anything I just packed my stuff up and left because I did not want to deal with that whole mess. That right there was just too much drama even for me. After this woman broke me and my man up she continued to pursue me for a couple more years. Then finally she found herself a girlfriend. I was so glad because I assumed she would move on but can you believe that nut started bringing her girlfriend around me to try and make me jealous. "Are you serious"? I never wanted this woman in the first place so there was no way she could make me jealous. Finally, when she realized nothing she was doing was going to work I guess she got the picture. She got the message that I had been trying to tell her for years. "I do not want you"! What we did together was just a crack thing now it was over, finished, and done. Crack addiction ain't no joke.

    I thank God for His deliverance every time I think about my life. I should have never taken that first hit of crack. I took that ride then the devil said move over because now I am going to drive. That is why I admonish everyone, every person not to let the devil drive. If you do he will take over. As an addict I went to places I never wanted to go and I did things I never wanted to do. I did whatever it took to get my next high. I remember I once posed in the nude with other women. I did it because I was a freak for crack. I worked as a call girl for a while too. If someone called I came and did everything it took to get a hit. As call girl I entertained men like doctors and lawyers. When you are a call girl you don't have to hit the streets to find a trick you are usually set up with a room and the men you service ask for you. I had many men who wanted only me because I was that good to them.

There was a lot of money to be made as a call girl. I remember this one guy who owned a casino. He would pay up to a thousand dollars to have me. I don't even think I would be with him for thirty minutes either. I wanted to get all the money I could from him so I got other girls to join in with me when he wanted to see me. When this guy would pay us I would keep half of the girl's money and my money as well. One time the man got robbed by some people who set him up. Everybody knew he had a lot of money so it was inevitable that he would eventually get robbed. He could not call the police on anyone because it would have ruined him. He would have been embarrassed and humiliated. That is how it goes with men who are high profile. I continued to service this same man for about three years. I made some good money off of him too.

III

All Cracked Out

I REMEMBER THIS one time I had been out smoking crack for several days. I had left my children with my sister. My sister knew I was out getting high because when I was nowhere to be found, I was getting high. My family knew all about my disappearing acts. When a person is an addict time really does not matter to them. The only thing I really cared about was enjoying my high and having fun. I would only come to my senses when the money ran out and no more crack was available. Then I would think about my main priorities like my children and my family. Somebody should have hit my across the head with a big stick. My sister was so tired of me popping in and out. I remember that night when I had left the crack house I went to my sister's house to go get my two daughters. I staggered to the door all doped up. I stood there and knocked like everything was normal. When my sister opened the door she took one look at me and saw I was high. "Nice of you to finally drop in" she said to me in a nasty tone. "Why you trippin" I said. I ain't trying to hear all that give me my babies so we can go." My sister looked at me with disgust and she would not let my girls leave with me. She saw me as an unfit mother. Really I was but I would never admit it. My sister and I exchanged some choice words and some insults, then I told her those were my children and I was going to take them with me regardless of what she said or what she thought about me. She still would not let me have my children. Finally we got into a fight which resulted in her calling the police on me. When the police arrived my sister told them I was high and she wasn't sure if I would take care of my kids or protect them properly. She also told the police that I was a crack addict and she felt I was in no shape to take them in my condition. I was furious with her. "How you gone put me on "Front Street" like that, I thought?" I could have scratched her face off. One thing a crack addict will hardly ever do is admit they smoke crack. I have heard people admit they smoked weed or snorted coke like they were proud of it but I've never heard a crack addict boast about being a crack head. You see crack is a very degrading drug. It is associated with filth and poverty. It is like when you get so low that there is nothing else for you get but crack. Drugs like cocaine and weed have been glamorized by Hollywood and people don't mind talking about it but a drug like crack is portrayed as the lowest of the low. I guess that is why it is called crack because you always want to hide a crack. Now how in the world can anyone categorize a drug? It is as ridiculous as trying to categorize sin. Every sin has to have the blood of Jesus to be forgiven or else it leads to death and destruction. That is why I can't understand people thinking they are better than someone else because they feel they have done lesser sins. We are all in the same boat when it comes to sin because no one can save themselves from the penalty of sin. And just like with addicts an addiction is an addiction and they all kill, steal, and destroy. Now that night that my sister called me out I was very upset. To me it wasn't anybody's business if I smoked crack or not. It is amazing how when you know you are guilty of an accusation it makes you so angry to hear it. The police officer looked at me and he told me that my children did not have to go with me just because I was their mother. He said to me, almost like he was sad, that they could decide for themselves if they wanted to stay with my sister or go home with me. I got cocky then. I was like "good let them decide who they want to go with." I was thinking to myself "now sis you think you know so much but you don't know nothing." I knew my sister was about to be embarrassed and I was going to gloat over it like a three year old singing the nah, nah, nah, nah, nah song. I just knew my babies were going to say they wanted to go with their mommy. Well I was totally clueless as to how they felt. I was so busy getting high all the time that I didn't know anything. I constantly blew them off for the crack pipe yet in my mind I thought I was a good mother. Crack will make you think you are a good everything. Crack is a deceiver. The truth is no addict is a good mother. An addict's commitment and loyalty is only to the drug they are enslaved to. Until I realized how sad I really was I thought everyone else had a problem except me. When my daughters made their choice to my surprise and shame they chose to stay with my sister and not go home with me. I was just stunned. I mean I was devastated. That hurt me so deeply that they chose her over me. I felt like I wanted to die on the inside. I burst into tears and boohooed from my soul. What could I have done, my babies had shut me out like I had shut them out. No one felt sorry for me or tried to console me and in my mind my sister had won. I left and walked down the street without my own children. I felt empty. When I got home the emptiness was even greater. I looked around the house; I sat down and I listened. There was not a sound. I didn't hear any laughter or playing. There was no movement, no noise, there was nothing. I had no one to love me neither did I have a shoulder to cry on. All my devotion to crack had me at an all-time low. I started to get angry I mean furious. Instead of taking responsibility for my behavior and making a change in my life I decided to blame everyone else for what had happened. I wallowed in self-pity. If I would have had any sense I would have gotten myself some help so I could mend the relationship with my daughters. But the addiction was so strong in me that even the pain and rejection I felt from that whole situation was not enough to make me stop smoking crack. Crack made me feel it was my only friend. I thought "I may as well smoke and get high because no one cares about me anyway". That was my excuse to justify my addiction. So after I convinced myself that everyone else was wrong except me I went and got high again. This time when I got high I felt depressed instead of satisfied. I started complaining to myself and "singing the blues". "How could my children not want to be with me, their own mother"? "I'm the one who really loves them". "They don't love me anymore and it's all my sister's fault". My thoughts were all prompted by crack craziness. The truth was my children loved me and they really wanted their mother. They just did not want me to be the way I was, a crack addict. Whenever I reflect back on those days I realize it must have been so scary for my girls. They never knew if I was dead or alive. When I was missing for days at a time, they did not know if I had abandoned them or not. They did not know if someone would harm them because I owed them money. They never knew if I would hallucinate and do something crazy to them. They had to have a lot of strength to deal with the life I created for them. All children want to feel safe and secure. They want some stability but that was something I never gave my girls. They never knew what to expect from one day to the next. I wanted to hold a grudge against my sister and the whole world but the real culprit in my life was me. I was the problem and I made it that way all by myself.

 I do not understand how crack had so much power over me that it could strip all the maternal love from me that I should have expressed to my children. I should have been the one they looked to for their needs to be met. I should have been the one to love them and build their self-esteem. I should have been a mother but instead I chose to be an addict. Later in my life God restored the love in me. Now that my girls are grown I find myself trying to give my grandchildren the kind of nurturing that I should have given them. The bible says if you resist the devil he will flee from you. (James 4:7) To resist means to stand firm against anything he throws your way. I needed to run from crack and get away from it but instead I was allowing it to destroy the ones I loved the most, my children, two of the most wonderful little girls in the world. I thank God that I learned before it was too late how to resist the devil and sin. God has transformed my mind. The bible has the answer to every problem we may encounter in this life. We cannot lose with the word of God. I can now look in the mirror and see how God has made a difference in my life. I am sending a message all over the world to let every person know God can bring you out. He is the one who is there for you when no one else gives a care, not crack. Crack is just a tool that the devil uses and nothing more.

IV

No Rescuer

I REMEMBER ONE day I was in the crack house smoking with people I thought I were friends. Isn't it amazing how birds of a feather flock together? Now that I am clean I see through all that "friends" stuff. I had no friends we all used each other to get high. I was trying to lay low this day because certain people were looking for me. I think they wanted to kill me. See there was this guy who had been injured so badly that he had to be hospitalized. His friends and family thought I had something to do with what had happened to him. Someone told them that I had caused the whole problem and I was responsible for all his injuries. His family had not spoken to me about anything they just believed what they heard on the streets. I had been set up and since everybody knew I was an addict whatever was said about me was just accepted whether it was true or not. I was guilty by association of crack. The man's family started searching for me all over the city. They even offered bribes to people pleading with them to tell where I was hiding. Well I hid out for a while but eventually I had to get my high on so I went to the crack house. When I got there I thought I was smoking with some people I could trust. Everybody was glad to see me so I let my guard down around them. That was a bad move on my part. I should have known I could never trust another addict. An addict will turn his own mother in for a hit. I thought I was amongst my friends but my friends ratted me out. I remember we were all sitting in the house smoking. I was feeling good because it had been a while since I had a hit. I forgot all my troubles. It was like Christmas in July when all of a sudden somebody grabbed me and started pushing me towards the door. I didn't realize what was going on. I was thinking "hold up yall I still got some crack to smoke." I did not know I had been set up and betrayed by my own so called buddies. They threw me out of the crack house into the streets so the people who were looking for me could catch me. Can you believe those addicts turned on me for a crack rock? Not for a car or some money, not for a medal of honor or a picture in the newspaper, no they turned on me for a crack rock. When those people got a hold of me they began to beat me like I was a run-away slave or something. They didn't just hit me with their fists no they hit me with car jacks, and sticks and empty beer bottles. Whatever they could get their hands on was what they used to beat me. One person even had a piece of a car bumper hitting me with it. Now where in the world did they find that to pick up and use? It was crazy. I was trapped by all those angry people and they were beating me all up and down the street. I was trying to get away but there were too many of them beating me. They beat me and beat me all over my body. I kept trying to get away. I know I punched somebody and clawed somebody too. They still beat me down though. I struggled and crawled until I had struggled enough to finally reach my house. People were coming out of their houses to see the beating. They watched the beat down but they sure did not bother to stop it. Now where were the people with their video cameras when I was getting assaulted? I could have been on TV saying "can't we all just get along." My family did not even know I was the one who was being attacked because I was completely surrounded with this gang of people beating the crap out of me. I knew I was going to die that day because I couldn't defend myself against all those people. I was high too and when you are high you really don't have that much strength. I couldn't do much of anything. I had to lie there and take that beating until finally a police car pulled up and broke up the ordeal. When the police got everybody off me blood was everywhere. My face was literally unrecognizable and I had bruises all over my body. I remember all the pain I felt. I was limping and I could not see out of but one eye. My hair was all messed up and I couldn't find one of my shoes either. It's a wonder that every bone in my body wasn't broken. One of the officers asked me if I wanted to go to the hospital and press charges. I told him no. I did not want to press charges because I was and addict and I was afraid. I felt like the police wouldn't do anything anyway. I would wind up dead on the streets somewhere. That is one of the rules of the dope game you never snitch. That will get you killed quicker that anything. I asked the officer to take me to my mother's house. The officer took me to her house and when she opened the door and looked at me she was horrified. She could not deal with me and my crack anymore. This was the last straw. She looked at me with no sympathy and told me without any hesitation "No, you can't stay at my house". Just like that my own mother shut me out and I had nowhere to go. She had to use tough love on me that day. So there I was. I had one shoe, a bloody face, my hair was messed up, I could hardly see out of my one good eye I had left, and worst of all I did not even get a chance to get my last hit at the crack house. That was a bad day for Myra believe me. The officers had to take me to a rehabilitation facility because if they would have left me on the streets ain't no telling what would have happened to me. It was not long after that incident that the people who had beaten me found out that they had the wrong person. I was beaten almost to death and turned on by my own mother for something I did not even do. That is the way it is for an addict. In the dope game anything goes. I was glad God had spared my life but I still continued to smoke crack even more. All I could think about while I was in rehab was going back on the streets to get high again. If I could have gotten away to a better environment after I was released I could have stayed clean. Many addicts have nowhere to go after rehab but back to the same places and the same people they left. I had a chance to get clean and move on with my life but I went back to the same environment and I keep getting high. Why was I still getting high? I can't tell you. Crack was never good for me. Many times I had nowhere to go and nowhere to live. I slept on people's front porches and their back porches because I was high. Sometimes I did not even know where I was. I used abandoned cars to sleep in and I slept in alley ways. I was always in danger because anyone could have harmed me. Can you imagine walking past an old abandoned car and seeing a woman lying there? First thought to probably come into your mind would be "crack head". My family wanted very little to do with me during those days and I really could not blame them. A person who has an addiction is a drain on everyone, especially those who have a relationship with them. I was a mess but you could not tell me that. I thought I was in control but I wasn't. My passion now is to help addicts come out of bondage. I know how hard it is to get free from crack. Some addicts get clean and sober but they wind up right back on the drug they left. I know it is because they have nowhere to go. To stay free from crack or any other drug a person has to first severe all associations form their past. You have to leave the "friends" alone and stay away from the places you once hung out. I have been clean for seven years and I still cannot go and sit with addicts at the crack house. The problem for most addicts who come out of rehab is they have no place to start anew. They have no money and no job so they find themselves right back where they were. It reminds me of a hamster on a wheel. Always moving but going nowhere. I want to let churches and support groups know how urgently help like this is needed.

V

Three Marriages

I WAS MARRIED three times. All of my marriages were abusive and crack always played the biggest part with the abuse. The beginning of my first marriage was wonderful, but after twelve years things took a turn for the worst. I allowed crack cocaine to come in and ruin my whole relationship. Let me start at the beginning, you see my mother raised me in a church going environment. She always quoted Proverbs 22:6 which say train up a child in the way he should go and when he is old he will never depart. I embraced the Christian background that my mom had instilled in me and when I grew up I married a minister of the gospel. My husband and I lived in Barstow, California. We traveled all over the country and did evangelistic work together. We also had a church with a congregation of over fifty members. My husband was the pastor and I was the first lady. We had an awesome ministry where we witnessed many miracles like people coming out of wheelchairs and healing of sickness. There was this one person at our church who was healed of cancer and someone else even had their limbs to grow out. Our ministry was incredible and on the move. We had sat under the ministry of a well know pastor who has a church in Crenshaw, CA. We were taught to live by faith and the word of God.

My husband and I also opened a boy's home for troubled youth with behavioral problems. I used to cook the meals and I was the house mother. I washed the boy's clothes and nurtured them like they were my own children. My husband was more a mentor to them. Things for us were going so well we seemed to have it all. Then my husband began to backslide. He started doing things that he knew were wrong. I could not understand what was going on with him. I confronted him a few times about his actions and I told him that he needed to get his act together so the ministry would not suffer but he did not listen to me. God will always privately warn you of what you are doing before things are exposed and you have open shame. My husband did not think he needed to listen to me because I was a woman but the bible says pride goes before destruction and a haughty spirit before a fall. (Proverbs 16:18) He got caught up in his own mess and brought a reproach on our church which closed down due to mismanagement. After the church closed we moved to Los Angeles and this is where everything spiraled downhill. My husband started drinking. Then his drinking led to smoking crack and weed. As things got worse and more worse we eventually had to close our boys' home. Then we lost the ministry and the church. I was very disappointed with my husband in the beginning and I resisted his lifestyle for a long time but it was not long before I got caught up in it too. Peer pressure is a powerful influence at any age. I started selling drugs and smoking weed right along with my husband to make fast money. It wasn't long after my husband started drinking and smoking weed that he got addicted to crack cocaine. That is what set it all off. Then I, like a dummy, followed right along in his footsteps. The addiction caused us to argue all the time. Most of the arguments were over crack, sex, adultery, and money. Little by little the arguing turned from verbal abuse and accusations to outright physical abuse. I went into my marriage expecting it to last my entire lifetime but the crack addition made that impossible. All of the faithfulness and commitment we once shared flew right out of the window and we started to lose everything. I remember this one night my husband and me got sprung (by sprung I mean really high). We were half out of it and not thinking straight so we decided we should sell all of our possessions and move away from California. I don't know where we thought we were going. Since we had been successful in life up until that point we had expensive furniture, and appliances, and jewelry. We told ourselves that we needed to move so we could do better but we knew we just wanted money to get high. After we had sold all our possessions guess what? We used the money to buy crack. Our addiction caused us to lose it all. What we did to ourselves made no rational sense and we continued to spiral out of control even more. One night my husband had a fit of rage because I refused to share some of my crack with him. As a result of that he beat me very badly. I never filed charges against him either. I wanted to leave him but I didn't because I needed more and more money for crack. We both liked getting high so we looked for ways to get the crack we craved. After we had basically sold everything we had, we had nothing left of real value but my wedding rings. So my husband insisted we sell them too. My rings were very expensive because like I said we had been in a prosperous season of our lives and the things we possessed were very nice. I really didn't want to sell my rings. They meant so much to me. I knew that if I didn't sell the rings it would lead to a fight and I didn't want him to beat me. I gave the rings to my husband and he sold them. Those rings were certainly worth more than we got for them. Our crack addiction caused us to lose physically, financially, and socially. I got to tell you crack ain't no joke.

Some family members moved in with my husband and me at the time that we were full blown addicts. They were addicts also so you can only imagine how crazy that situation was. One day we were smoking and I didn't want to share my crack. Let me explain, see in the crack game you like to have someone to smoke with but if you smoke with the same people over and over you get tired of them. I was tired of these relatives and I would make up excuses why I couldn't let them have any of my crack. That particular day I told them I had used my last few dollars and I only had just enough crack for me to get high. I was lying though; I had gotten a check that morning. They knew I had a check but I told them that someone stole my check. I pretended to be upset so they wouldn't be suspicious. I accused everyone in the house of stealing the check. My husband, not knowing what I was doing, became furious. He put everyone out of the house and called them a bunch of thieves. When a person is an addict even if they tell the truth no one believes them. I got my relatives kicked out with no place to go just so I could have the entire check to buy crack for myself. When they left I showed my husband the check. No one apologized to the relatives, we just immediately went and cashed that check and got high. Crack makes you very selfish. It blocks your ability to have compassion. All it does is drive you to do anything you can to get another hit. I should have been able to help my relative overcome their addiction. I say that because I was raised in church and I had even witnessed the power of God in a mighty way but I was too busy getting high myself to help anyone else. My relatives eventually moved back in with us and the addiction grew worse and worse. This time they were there I stole my father-in-laws' television set and my mother-in laws' furniture. I staged the whole thing like it was a robbery but my father-in-laws had me arrested. I staged the robbery so good that no one could pin it on me. No charges were filed against me so I got away with the crime. My husband was gone when this happened. When he got home he was very upset over what I was accused of so he kicked everybody out again. When our relatives left we had nothing in our house because we had sold all our furniture. All we had basically was each other and a crack addiction. We were the type of family you read about in magazines. We went from rags to riches and it happened so fast. We set a horrible example for the Christian community, our families, and our children but none of that mattered to us at that time because crack had us bound and we did not know how to get out. We did a complete turnaround from holiness to worldliness. Once the devil got his foot in the door, and we allowed him to, he had a field day with our lives. Our marriage ended in divorce and it really did not have to be that way. Today my ex-husband is clean and back in the ministry. He is again a mighty man of God.

My second husband was an addict just like my first husband. We would often get high together and think nothing of it. He was very abusive to me too. I still to this day wonder how I survived him. I know God was with me even then. I remember this one time I had left home to go get high. I was gone for about a week and no one knew where I was. You might think how can a wife and mother stay away from home a whole week unaccounted for? Well that's the way the crack game goes. I was out smoking crack and I did not think about my family or myself; I just wanted to get high. I remember this incident so well because when I did return home I tried to get in the door and to my surprise I could not get in. Someone had changed the locks and that someone was my husband. I was so angry at myself for having stayed away so long. I knocked on the door and no one let me in. I knew my husband was home but I couldn't figure out why he wouldn't open the door. I kept knocking and knocking and no one answered. "Oh, it's on now, I thought." I knew he was home so I was really ticked off by then. I found this jack from a car and I picked it up and used it to knock down the door. I probably shouldn't have knocked down the door but I wanted to know why my husband was tripping. I mean how you gone change the locks on me. I was only gone for a few days. This is how I rationalized the situation in my mind. In the crack game you always want to blame everyone else for the things you bring on yourself. After I broke down the door things went from bad to worse because when I confronted my husband about changing the locks I got the shock of my life. Not only had he changed the locks on me but he had replaced me with another woman . . . and this woman was someone I knew! I was just stunned, I couldn't believe it. As I think back on this incident I just shake my head. There are no rules in the crack game. It's every man for himself and if you get played in the process, oh well. Not only did I feel betrayed and hurt by my husband but he added insult to injury by humiliating me even more. He told me he was with this woman because she performed good oral sex. Right in front of her like she was so special. He told me I should learn some skills from her because she knew how to satisfy a man. Was he kidding? He had no idea that I was better at oral sex than her. I was the master when it came to that. She couldn't teach me anything. If he only knew the things I learned on the streets so I could get my next high it would send chills through his body. As a matter of fact I was good at everything because I did it all but I never told him that. We went back and forth at each other through the night arguing but by the time morning came we were getting high together. It's kind of funny now to me and sad at the same time that no matter how bad any situation got with us we always found a way to get a high out of it. I don't know if we came to an agreement over the other woman or not. I just remember that we were all smoking and having a good time when all of a sudden my husband rose up and hit me up side my head with a cowboy boot. I don't know what got into him. One minute everything was fine then the next minute he was like a maniac. He began to beat me, and beat me, and beat me. I guess he thought about me having been gone for a week or maybe the crack had some kind of effect on his brain whatever it was that man beat me like crazy. I don't know why I didn't end up in the hospital or why he didn't wind up in jail. Nevertheless, I was abused and no one suffered any consequences and no charges were filed either. After he beat me so badly I had to leave him for a while. I returned later but I hardly ever stayed at home. I was in and out all the time. I'd stay out on crack binges for several days or even weeks then I would go back to him. I was more like a guest then a wife. Things were never the same in our marriage after the beatings started. When a man beats you it takes something out of you. It's like a part of your spirit is bruised. This marriage was destroyed and there were three of us to blame for it me, my husband, and crack cocaine. One night I dropped in after having been gone for I'd say about maybe a week or two. I probably had run out of money. I remember my husband was getting ready to go out. He did as he pleased and I did too. There was no commitment with us. I could tell he was high. I was good and high too so when we talked to each other we got into an argument. The argument soon turned into a fight. We would often fight all over the house. This time the fight wound up in our bedroom. I was standing beside the bed fussing and screaming at him. The bed had four sharp posts that stuck up on each corner. That made the bed room not the best place for two high people to fight. We began to fight each other like crazy. All of a sudden my husband pushed me and I fell face forward towards the bed. I tried to catch my fall but I was high and my coordination was off. I fell right into one of those sharp posts. The post pierced me directly through my eye. It was so painful I'm surprised I didn't black out or lose my eye. Blood began to gush out all over the room. It was like a scene from a horror movie. I could have been blinded but I know God intervened for me. I must have gone into shock because I don't remember how we stopped the bleeding. My husband did not know what to do. He was all scared and paranoid. He didn't want to take me to the hospital because he was high. On top of that I was high too. Worst of all he knew he had caused the accident and he knew he was in hot water. I really can't remember all the details of that night but I know I wound up at the hospital somehow. Someone dropped me off and left. No one took the time to stay with me and make sure I was okay. There I was by myself all bloody and disoriented. That is the way it is when you're an addict. A doctor came in and examined me in the emergency room. He was rather testy when he asked me what happened. I told him about the fight with my husband. I told him it was an accident but he just sort of blew me off. After that some people on the hospital staff came in and urged me to call the police and press charges against my husband. I didn't want to press charges against him because I did not know what would happen to me. He was violent and crazy and I never knew what to expect from him. After much coercion I was convinced to file the charges so I did. I reluctantly gave my statement to the authorities. When I was discharged I called my husband to come and pick me up. He arrived at the hospital and was arrested. I cannot begin to tell you how angry he was with me. I was nervous and afraid at first but when I thought about all the beatings and abuse I didn't care. That was what he deserved anyway. It felt good to have some justice done for me for me for a change. I should have let my husband learn a lesson from that arrest by doing some time but I didn't. I couldn't. I wound up dropping the charges and do you know why? I didn't drop the charges because I loved and cared about him. I didn't drop the charges because I wanted to get him back and work our marriage through. No, I only dropped the charges because he was one of my crack suppliers and I knew I would need him one day for a hit. My desire for crack made me think I needed him like that so I thought "why mess up a good thing"? Crack was my only motivation and I put it above my own safety and self-respect. I took the abuse and even faced death just to get high. Even though this marriage was a disaster, I must tell you that today my ex-husband is clean and he is a saved man of God. I praise God for his deliverance. After I left husband number two for good I met another man and married him. This was husband number three. I thought this marriage was going to be different but it wasn't. I found it to be the same old thing. He smoked crack just like I did. We were both addicts. This husband started out verbally abusing me. He would tell me I was nothing and he would humiliate me in front of my friends. He would say "You will never be nothing but a crack head and a whore." I don't know why I would let him say those things to me because he was no better than me. He was a crack head and he whored around just as much as I did. Many times men sell themselves the same way women do when they are addicts. I was so messed up by this time that I stayed in that marriage even though it was awful. After a while, just like before, this husband also began to physically abuse me. He would strangle me and beat me all the time. He would take me to isolated places way out in the country or in a wooded area and he would threaten me. He would tell me how he could kill me or mutilate me and hide my body and no one could ever find me. He would keep me in those isolated areas for hours and hours. Sometimes there would be mosquitoes biting me. I mean they would literally eat me up. If I complained to him about it he would say "so, I don't care". I think he got a rush out of having control and power over someone. He would jump at me with his hands raised like he was about to hit me just to see me cringe. Sometimes I would get on my knees and beg my husband not to hurt me or kill me. I would say anything to get him to stop scaring me. I would tell him I loved him and that I couldn't live without him. One time he took me out to this isolated place like the middle of nowhere. I don't know where it was. He made me get out of the car and he left me there. I was terrified. There were no light and no houses. I was walking aimlessly trying to find someone to help me. I walked and walked for hours until I found some help. When I finally made it home he acted like he had not done anything wrong. I was so mad at him but I didn't do anything. I was afraid to. I was more afraid in this marriage that in any of the others. Since nothing was said or done we both went and got high together. Getting high was the only thing I had at that time that made sense in my life. That is how bad things were. I used to never say anything to him about the way he treated me but after I got clean and started living for God I became bold and confident and little by little I began to stand up for myself. One time my husband choke-slammed me into our living room wall. He shoved me so hard that it left my body print in the wall. This particular night I had gone out to pick up some crack but I ended up smoking most of it before I got home. When my husband found out that I had smoke all the crack without him he just lost it. He started yelling at me and calling me all kinds of dirty names. Then he hauled off and hit me. After that he slammed me into the wall holding me by the neck. My oldest daughter was there so she called the police. When the police arrived they saw the body print in the wall and they could not believe it. I am sure they wanted to laugh because now that I think about it that is kind of funny. It was like a scene from a cartoon having the print of my body slammed into the wall. My daughter hit my husband on the side of his head with a skillet but I did not want her to get involved. I was glad she did however because I was high and I really could not fight him. My balance was off and I was incoherent. My daughter asked him to leave me alone but he wouldn't. He was just a beating and beating on me. I did not want to fight in front of my daughter or my grandchildren, but thank God for that skillet that day.

It seemed like the police would come to our home almost every weekend when I was with husband number three. One time a police officer sat down with me and talked. I guess he felt sorry for me. He asked me why did I stay with that man and take all of those beatings and do you know what? I really could not answer him. I mean I wasn't in love with the guy and I didn't even have fun with him. We had nothing in common. He was mean and self-centered and he treated me bad all the time. I did all I could to get along with him. Now, I realize I was only with him because I needed him to get the crack I used to get high. I remember after I got clean and started attending church my husband used to hate it. He once told me that he was the devil then he did this evil laugh in a deep voice. He said, "ha, ha, ha". He said the devil had assigned him to me. Sometimes when I would go to church he would send people to come in and get me. He did that just to be mean. Once I got clean I never went back to doing the things I did when I first met my husband. I was determined to live holy and remain sold out for Christ. Then one day he told me that since he could not change me back into a crack addict it was time for him to leave and that was just what he did. It was during that period of my life that I began to take an inventory of myself and I realized that every relationship I had gotten into was horrible. I thought maybe someone had put a curse on me or something. That was my lot in life, three failed marriages and nothing to show for it. Was I in love with any of my husbands? Were they in love with me? I honestly don't know the answer to those questions. What I do know without a doubt is that God loves me and it was not His will for me to go through all the hell I went through. Back then I didn't know what to do or who I could turn to. Now I know God has the answer for every problem. Any woman who is in an abusive relationship or marriage let me tell you there is a way out. You don't have to take anything you don't like. I stayed in the abuse with my husbands for crack. I didn't believe I had a choice. I can't stress enough to you how much addiction will affect a person's self-esteem. Abuse that the average person wouldn't tolerate becomes what an addict begins to feel they deserve. I guess I had to get tired enough of my situation to do something about it. I did divorce husband number three and I do believe God broke whatever curse was on my life also. When I divorced him I decided to let God heal me inside and out. I stopped dating or even seeing anyone for about three years. I am still happily single even now because I choose to be. I had to let my mind and my body heal. I thank God for His power and I praise Him for all He has done in my life. Even though I had an addiction and I was at my lowest, no man had the right to abuse me or degrade me. It does not matter whether I am an addict or clean I am still a child of God and I was not put here for abuse. Yes, I stayed in abuse and addictions for a long time but remember what I said before, you don't have to stay in anything. God does not want anyone to be in bondage like the bondage I was in. He brought me out and gave me this testimony so He can have all the glory. God wants you to be free.

VI

In Harm's Way

I REMEMBER THIS one time I smoked so much that I ended up in the emergency room. I was taking a hit as usual when I started having chest pains. My whole chest began to tighten and I felt like I was about to die. No one would help me or give me a ride to the hospital. The addicts I was smoking with were probably afraid that I was playing some game so I could rob them. When it comes to crack anything can happen. I wound up having to crawl about three blocks to the hospital. I used all the energy I had in me to crawl because I was determined that I was not going to die like that. When I got to the hospital I was having an irregular heart beat and my blood pressure was very high. I was given oxygen because I could not catch my breath. This was all a result of crack use. My family did not want to come to the hospital to check on me. They were sick and tired of me using them. I could not blame them either because I was tired of myself. My husband and sister did wind up coming however. They did not come because they were concerned. They came to find out if I had spent all the food stamps on my food stamp card. They were asking me questions and I could hear what they were saying but I could not respond to them. I was sedated. I could hear them talking about me like a dog. It hurt my feelings so much. When I left the hospital no one came to pick me up so I went back to the same crack house that I had crawled from. Crack was right there waiting on me and yeah I smoked it again. I said to myself "No one cares about me anyway so I may as well smoke." That was my crutch to justify getting high. I almost died yet that was not enough to make me give up crack. The addiction was that strong in me. Like I said it can literally destroy you. If I had known taking that one hit out of curiosity would have led to the destruction of my life believe me I would have never done it. Don't be deceived by the devil. If you try it it will happen to you. It took nineteen years of my life to correct a fifteen minute decision.

I remember one time I left home at about 7:30 in the morning and from about 7:30a.m. until about 3:00a.m. I was getting high. When my money had run out I knew I had to get my hustle on to get some more crack. I wanted to continue in my high so I left the crack house searching for anything or anyone who had drugs. When a person wants crack it seem like the devil makes a way for them to get it. While I was on that binge I ran into one of my daughter's friends. This friend began to talk to me about how I was hurting my daughter. He told me I should go home and get off the streets. He explained to me how worried my family was and how I needed to be there for them. Even though this guy was right, he irritated me because he was bringing down my high. I let his words fly out of my mind. The only thing I could think about was getting high. I even wondered if maybe he could be the source of my next high. After he said what he had to say I told him he needed to move on because he was blocking my hustle. Deep down inside I felt horrible because I know he was telling me right. He was telling me the truth but I didn't listen. I mean how could I? I didn't want to be the way I was but I was caught up at that point and those who got hurt were just casualties of crack. Addiction always makes you feel like you have no choice and no way out. That night while I was out making money and getting high I kept hearing the words that my daughter's friend had spoken to me. I tried to block them out so I wouldn't have to face myself but I couldn't. Why was he in my business anyway, I thought? Didn't he know I had this under control? I could stop and go home any time I wanted to. That's what I told myself so that guilt and shame would not consume me. The truth was I didn't have control of anything. Crack had control of me. I stayed out three more nights after that because I was afraid to go home and face my family. The looks of disappointment and disgust were too much to bear. I was ashamed of me and what I was doing. I was stinking because I had not taken a bath in days. I was dirty. I mean have you ever seen a clean crack house. I was hungry. I was too busy getting high who had time to eat? I was "toe up from the flo' up". Crack cocaine will make a person forget all about personal hygiene and appearance. Then after they come off the high reality will set in. This is when a person realizes what a "hot mess" they are. I decided not to go home so I stayed in the streets a few more days. This time while I was out I ran into this guy I knew very well. He wanted to get high as much as I did so we hooked up and found us some crack. I wish I would have listened to sound wisdom and gone home like my daughter's friend had advised me to but oh no, not me. I was an addict and I was not about to let an opportunity to get high pass me by. I went with the guy to his house that night because I considered him to be a good buddy of mine and I trusted him. We started smoking and we were having a good time. I had no reason to fear him because we had smoked together before. What he did next caught me totally off guard. He jumped up and punched me in the chest so hard that he knocked the wind out of me. I started coughing and wheezing; I couldn't breathe. After I regained my composure I was puzzled. What had I done wrong, I thought? I asked him what in the world was wrong with him. He grabbed me and told me that he had wanted sex from me for quite a while and since we were alone he was going to get it. I was repulsed. You want to do what? I just wanted to get high. I was not in the game to turn tricks for free. Especially with this loser, this was more than I had bargained for. He then began to rape me and there was nothing I could do. If I went to the police they wouldn't help. I was known as a crack prostitute. They would say I was turning a trick to get high. No charges were filed and nothing was done to him. I was so hurt. I felt violated and betrayed. I felt like I had no control, no dignity, and no respect. I began to cry. After he had finished his business I sat there not knowing what to do. I should have picked up something and knocked him out. I should have gone and gotten some of my crew to beat him down. I should have got out of there too but I didn't. That's right; I stayed there with him like a dummy. That is how crazy the addiction was. I was strung out on crack and I needed to get high so I stayed there and continued to smoke with him even after he had just raped me. It seemed to happen all the time that no matter how bad a situation was I always managed to get a high out of it. When I left that man's house I kept thinking about the rape. I could not believe he did that to me. Not him. How could he be so callus? The more I thought about the rape the more I needed to get high. I could not shake my grief and anger. I went to the house of a drug dealer that I knew and I told him what had happened. The drug dealer became irate because the guy who had raped me was his best friend. He told me that no one had the right to rape me no matter what I was or what I did. I should have known that already but I didn't value myself. Crack addiction takes away person's self-esteem, self-value, and self-worth. We talked for a while and I guess he felt sorry for me so he gave me some free crack. Big mistake, he must have forgotten I was a crack addict or maybe he felt responsible for his friend. Whatever the reason was it didn't matter to me. I began to tell him all kinds of sad stories to get more and more free crack. The more hits he gave me the more stories I came up with. It was pathetic. When I left his house I went home. I had probably been out for about three weeks straight. When I look back I wonder how I stayed alive. I did not eat hardly any food (crack makes a person crave crack not food). I remember I used to go to grocery stores and sneak grapes and lunch meat sometimes just to keep myself going. I would seldom have any meals. I could go four or five days without eating anything. I was so thin I looked like a skeleton. I probably thought I was sexy too. I was always outside exposed walking the streets or in some nasty house that was about to fall apart. I just wanted to get high. Nothing else was important to me. I know God is good because it was He that had mercy on me and protected me during that time of my life. You see crack am not no joke. I would not even introduce my worst enemy to crack. I know how it affected me and I would not want to see anyone strung out like that. Crack will make a person do things that they would never do otherwise.

I remember this time I stole a thousand dollars from someone that I was close to and really loved. I remember I took the money to the crack house and started smoking like I was a millionaire. I had all my so called buddies with me. I wanted to impress them so I splurged and showed off by spending big bucks. I told them how slick I was and how I had stolen all the money I had. I was feeling like I was somebody special. And my friends acted like I was the best thing since sliced bread. After I had smoked for a while I became selfish about sharing my crack. I began to think "hey, I was the one who stole this money". Those crack addicts were trying to smoke up my entire stash of crack and I wasn't having that. I decided I wanted to get high by myself so I lied and told all my friends that were smoking with me that I had run out of money. They got angry with me because they knew I was lying. I had already shown them the money when I was splurging and acting like a big shot. Why did I do that? I was an addict myself and I knew you couldn't let anyone know how much money you had. I was asking to get robbed. I was too busy trying to be a show off to think about that. I had a broken arm at the time and there was a cast on it. I don't think I had had that cast on for long either. Well that made no difference to anyone there because they actually broke the cast off my arm looking for my money. They were relentless. I kept telling them I didn't have any more money. They didn't know I had hid the money inside my body. I knew how to hide numerous things inside my body. I had to learn how to do things like that because in the crack game you really don't have any friends. The people you smoke with most of the time are just using you. And don't think for one minute a crack addict won't do you in. One minute everybody can be smoking and having a good time. Then in a split second the whole scene can change. When no one could find any money on me everybody there turned on me. They grabbed me and tied me to a chair. They weren't stupid. They knew I had done something with that money. They all began to question me. "Where's the money", they asked? I kept my story the same. It's all gone. Yall smoked it up. I don't have any more money. I didn't know if they would beat me, or kill me, or what. Finally, they got fed up with me and things got out of control. One guy threatened me by telling me that he was going to set me on fire. I guess everybody else was going to help him do it because no one protested. The guy said he was going to spray my body with hair spray and then ignite it with a cigarette lighter. I was horrified. I thought to myself "yall supposed to be my friends"? I was in a predicament and I had to do something fast. Luckily for me I was a hustler and I could basically talk my way out of just about anything. I started my fast talking, (by that I mean I started conning them). I told everybody that I had lied to them and that I had hid the money in another place. I told them that I was going to show them where I put it if they let me go. However, I was thinking to myself "if these fools let me go they'll never see me or that money". I don't know what I said that made them believe me. Didn't they know they couldn't trust an addict? Maybe they really wanted to get high. All I know is they cut me loose and told me to go get it. Two of the guys that were there said they were going to accompany me so I could give the money to them. Yeah right, like that was going to happen. They held me by the arms. When I got outside that crack house I broke loose from them and I ran like I was an Olympic champion. I went from zero to sixty in ten seconds. I didn't even know I could run so fast. I guess when your life is in danger it is amazing what you are capable of doing. They were chasing me but one thing about the dope game is that you will never catch an addict on the run. I made it out of that situation unharmed. Yes, I thank God that I did. I was very fortunate but I still continued to smoke crack. I just could not leave it alone.

    I remember this other time I was at the crack house getting high with my "friends" when all of a sudden someone kicked in the door. I thought it may have been the police or some undercover narcotics agent but it wasn't. It was a bunch of addicts. They rushed in with guns and lined everybody up. They demanded that we take off all our clothes. I mean every stitch; men and women. They did that to make sure no one had any weapons. Some of the addicts were probably already naked. That is what people often do in the crack house. I have been in crack houses where everybody got naked, freaked each other, and had orgies. Removing all my clothes was very degrading but I did as I was told because I didn't want to get killed. They robbed us and took everything we had of value, our jewelry, our money, and worst of all our entire stash of crack. So there I was buck naked with no crack. As an addict I thought "That is so messed up. Now I gotta go rob somebody to get me some more crack". I guess I did not realize it was just by the grace of God that no one got shot or killed. I think I was more upset over losing my crack than potentially losing my life. In the crack game you never know what to expect. After the addicts robbed us they left. All of us were upset. "What is this world coming to, I said to myself? "I can't believe they took our crack"! That's all it was about, crack. I remember I put my clothes back on and went to find some more crack to smoke. That near death experience was just the motivation I needed to feel sorry for myself so I could go get high some more. Yep, it was going to take more than that to get me to stop smoking my crack.

VII

Getting Money for Crack

DURING THE TIME I was an addict I had all kinds of ways to get money to get crack. I used to rob people and prostitute myself to get what I needed. I remember this time I had met this guy and he had a business recycling aluminum cans. He was a successful man and he always had money. One day he wanted me to turn a trick with him, (that means he wanted me to have sex with him for money). I agreed to do it and afterwards he paid me one hundred and fifty dollars. One hundred and fifty dollars is nothing to trade for persons' dignity and self-respect but I was a crack addict and I wanted to get high so hey I turned that trick with honors. After we finished business this guy made a big mistake. He let me, a crack addict; see where he kept the money from his business. I guess he thought he could trust me because I rocked his world with sex. Little did he know there is no trust with a crack addict. I have known women who have sold their own children to a drug dealer just to get a hit. When I saw all that money he had, my mind began to scheme. I said to myself "Oh yeah, he's got money in his shop and I'm gonna get it." It did not matter to me that this man treated me very well. All I thought about was easy money to get high with. That is exactly the way crack will influence you to think. I really didn't want to do this man wrong but when I saw that money the addiction took over. I robbed him and took all the money he had. I spent it on crack as fast as I could get to the crack house. It felt good to get high too because I didn't have to work to get that money. I had fun until I came down off my high. When I realized what I had done I felt dirty and low down. When you smoke crack it gives you a thrill at first but when reality sets in you feel so ashamed. The next day I went back to see this same guy whom I had just robbed and I acted like nothing had happened. I could tell he was suspicious of me. He told me he had been robbed. I acted like I was surprised. As an addict I learned to be a good liar and an academy award actress. He told me that I was the only person that had been in his shop. I didn't say a word. He could not really pin the robbery on me but I think he kind of knew. He never did ask me out right did I do it either. I guess he didn't want to jeopardize future tricks. He wasn't a crack addict. He only dealt with me because he liked the way I made him feel. After that he then gave me three hundred and fifty dollars. I was overwhelmed. I had treated him so wrong and he still was good to me. I didn't allow myself to feel bad about what I had done though; I was too busy making plans to go get high with that money he had just given me. Now that I am clean and I reflect back on him I realize that man was an addict also. No, he didn't smoke crack but he was bound by sex. We used each other to get our fixes. The addiction I had was making me vulnerable to dangerous situations. That man could have beaten me. I could have contracted an STD from him. He could have had me arrested too. I was doing things that were irresponsible and illogical. Inside I did not want to hurt anyone but my desire for crack took away any sympathy or compassion I could have shown anyone. When I was high I didn't care. My only ambition was to get higher and higher. It was shameful and disgraceful. I have to tell you again crack ain't no joke. I know God worked overtime to protect me while I was an addict.

I remember one time I went to a motel room with some of my friends, well I thought they were friends. We were smoking and I just couldn't seem to put the crack pipe down. I was insatiable. I kept smoking, and smoking, and smoking. I had no self-control. The crack had me. Finally, the friends I was smoking with became annoyed with me. I could look at their faces and tell but I thought we were cool like that so I kept on smoking. I guess I must have gone too far with the smoking that time, because it wasn't long before a couple of the guys there wanted me to perform for them, (by perform mean they wanted me to do some sexual acts for them). Were they crazy? I just wanted to get high. They began to pressure me. I got scared because I didn't know at that point if they would harm me or not. I was so high from smoking so much that I couldn't do anything anyway. I was totally wasted. One of the guys, or should I say one of the so called friends I was with, was not having that. He was ready to get serviced and he was fed up with me. He abruptly grabbed me and stuck a gun down my throat. He demanded that I do what he wanted me to do or else. I tried to comply so he wouldn't pull the trigger but I was literally so high that I could not perform. I tried to talk to him with the gun in my mouth. I was too high to grasp the severity or the moment. I asked him why he was tripping like that. I thought we were all good. I had smoked so much of his crack that he felt I owed him something. I was in over my head. There I was with all those angry addicts. They could have done anything they wanted to me and I would not have been able to do a thing about it. The guy that had the gun in my mouth pulled it away from me and he said "Either you turn some tricks or you pay for everything you smoked." I didn't have any money and they knew it. In the crack game people will set you up and when they do they can basically have their way with you because you owe them. I know God was protecting me that night. I convinced those guys to let me go. I told them I would go out and make some money and I would bring it straight to them. They must have been as high as I was or just plain stupid. They knew well and well that they couldn't believe anything an addict promised. When I left them they didn't see me anymore. I hid from them and every time I was somewhere getting high I would be nervous. I would always watch my back because I didn't know if they still had it in for me or what. I was all psyched out and scared to death. They never did find me either. Regardless of what had happened that still was not enough to stop me from smoking crack. No sir, a gun down my throat and my life having been threatened was not going to mess up my high. You see in the crack game anything goes. I didn't go to the police to have anyone arrested. The police wouldn't do anything anyway. Besides all that they might have arrested me. As a matter of fact the police there where I lived used to hate to see me coming. They knew my back ground. To them I was a just a crack prostitute, an addict, and a thief. I was only trouble to them; it didn't matter what happened to me. Sometimes they acted like they could have cared less. I have to keep this story real so I can let you know how despicable the crack world is. But no matter how bad a person is treated they must remember that God loves unconditionally. It was He who helped me even when I didn't know it. God sustained me through those years. I thought I was the worse whore, call girl, and prostitute that there was and because of the way I thought of myself I let people treat me any kind of way. Yes, I did things due to my addiction but God loved me even then. He looked past my condition and saw me. Sometimes it is hard for me to grasp all that I went through. I am amazed that I am still alive. I thank God that I never contracted AIDS or HIV. That in itself is enough for me to Praise Him. When I tell you I am sold out for Christ you better believe I AM SOLD OUT FOR CHRIST.

VIII

Driven by Crack

WHEN MY CHILDREN got older I lived with my oldest daughter. She knew I was an addict so she could not trust me like children who had clean parents could trust their parents. On rare occasions however she would trust me to drive her car to the grocery store. Sometimes I would take the car without her knowing. One time I took her car without her permission and I stayed out a long time. I went to the crack house and started smoking. When you are getting high it is so easy to lose track of time because you basically do not care about anybody's time but yours. I parked my daughter's car close to the crack house so when she came looking for me it was not hard for her to find me. She was very upset and needed her car but I had the keys. She came to the door of the crack house. I saw her as she was approaching so I told everybody I was smoking with to say I wasn't there. She yelled through the door "come out mama I know you're in there". Somebody in the crack house yelled back "she ain't here". She shook her head with frustration because she was tired. She kept yelling for me to come out. I began to get annoyed because she was messing up my high. I handed the keys to someone to give to her. I told them to tell her I had left the keys there by accident. Okay how dumb was I at that time. She saw her car parked by the crack house and she probably saw me in there too. I thought I was hidden so well. I remember I was peeping out the window and looking all paranoid. That is what crack does. Now I know my daughter had a lot of compassion because anyone else would have probably beaten me down for stealing their car. I remember her friends used to ask her about me and she would say "crack". If they asked "how is your mom", she would say "crack." They had this routine they would go through. They would say "What your mama look like"; she'd say "crack." "What your mama smell like, crack." "What your mama act like, crack." "What your mama doing, crack." My daughter would say crack to any question asked about me. I know she did it because she was embarrassed and fed up with me. She tried to make the hurt she was feeling inside into a game to hide her pain. I was so busy getting high back in those days that I really did not understand what I was doing to my children.

IX

A Victim of Rape

IN THE CRACK game there are many unfortunate things that happen that can destroy you more than the drug itself. I was raped over five times as an addict and each rape affected my life in a traumatic way. My first rape was like a nightmare. I remember I was out late at night looking for some crack to smoke when I ran into this guy I knew who had some money. He told me to go with him to his motel room so we could get high together. When we got to the motel room I thought I was going to get high and have a good time. I did not know that he had other things on his mind. We were not in the room a good ten minutes when he threw me down one the bed, jumped on top of me, and started tearing at my clothes. I started screaming and fighting him off of me, but he was too strong for me. He covered my mouth with one hand and told me to stop screaming or else. At that point I was hysterical and I kept crying and yelling for help. The man then grabbed me by the throat and began to choke me. He kept his hands so tight around my throat that I was at the point of death. I literally saw my life flash before my eyes. I saw myself as a child and my life as I was growing up. I even saw my own funeral and my family preparing for it. I then gave up struggling with him. He then took my clothes off and raped me. I do not even know how long it lasted or what sex with him was like because I separated from my conscience. I zoned out I guess my brain did that to protect me from losing my mind totally. When I came to the guy was gone and I was at the hospital. The guy had put a gold chain around my neck. I don't know what the chain was for? I guess he felt guilty over what he had done to me. All I know is when I became coherent again I had a chain around my neck. I don't even remember riding in the ambulance or talking to the police. I just remember I was at the hospital. My nose was bleeding and my mouth was swollen and bruised. The doctors said they could tell I had been strangled because there was a ring around my neck. I was in the hospital for hours. The police tried to get me to tell them who had done that to me but I would not give them a statement. I was afraid to because I was a crack addict. I felt like I had no rights. My self-value and self-esteem was so low that I maybe even felt I deserved to have something bad happen to me. Crack addiction will bring you to that point. I saddest part of all about my rape was that I took that necklace that the guy had given me and sold it. I then used the money to buy crack. It was the only thing at that point that could help me cope with the way I felt inside. Later on I told my brothers what happened and who it was that had raped me. They beat the guy up really bad and they continued to do so on many occasions. They wanted to teach him a lesson but no matter how many times they beat him it still could not take back what he had taken from me. I felt so helpless and so all alone. I was so messed up that I even thought about committing suicide. No matter how much I washed myself and how much I scrubbed it seemed like I could never get clean. It took the love of God to help me through that rape.

 The next rape made me feel like I was nothing. I was raped by two men and they treated me like I was trash. They humiliated me and made me feel like I was nobody when they got through with me. They were the maintenance men at the apartment complex where I lived. I used to sell drugs to them and they would come to freak parties that I used to host at different hotels. At the freak parties everybody fondled everyone else and had sex sometimes too. Everyone got high together and freaked. It was sort of like an orgy but we called them freak parties. This one particular party I threw I did not participate in any activity and these men got angry. They wanted to be with me because they had heard a lot about me. I was not interested in them I was only throwing those parties to make money. When the party was over I left and went home to my apartment. I was about to go to bed when I heard a knock at the door. When I opened the door to my surprise there were the two maintenance men. They forced their way through the door and grabbed me. Since they had been in my apartment before doing repairs they knew I kept a can of mace on top of my refrigerator. They got it and sprayed me with my own mace. I was screaming and I asked them what did they want? I thought they wanted to rob me because I had made a lot of money at the party. They said they want me to have sex with them. I knew they were high because we all go high at the party. I then realized they wanted to rape me. I grabbed the telephone and pressed zero. The operator got on the phone and she could hear the whole ordeal. The men held me down and I could not fight them off because I was high and I had no strength. They told me not to make a sound and they both began to rape me at the same time from the front and back. When they finished with me they asked me where my daughters were because they wanted to rape them too. I had sent my girls to stay with one of my friend that night so I could throw the freak party. I thank God I did that because if they had been home they would have been raped or maybe even killed. I really don't know. I could not even imagine my girls having to experience such devastation as a rape. Since the operator was on the phone and heard what was going on she called the police. When the police arrive they arrested the two men. Later on I found out my best friend had set up that whole nightmare. She was mad at me because I had slept with a guy who was a pimp. He was like the head pimp and she was in love with him. She got jealous of me because he showed an interest in me and not her. She arranged for me to be raped to get even. The pimp did punish her when he found out but that did not change what had happened nor did it make me feel any better. I began to ask myself "Why God, why me?" When I went to court I had to face those two men again. In that court room it felt like they were raping me all over again. I began to think back when I was small how a man used to tamper with me. I had to re-live all that pain and embarrassment again.

My third rape messed me up in my mind something terrible. It was so horrific that I will not even go into the details about it and crack was involved this time too. After this rape I began to hate men. No, not just some of them but all of them because I felt like they were all the same. I remember crying out to God. "Lord can I ever be loved"? When a person is raped it takes all your pride, dignity, and self-esteem. I began to isolate myself and sit in my house with no lights on very depressed. I remember one day my daughter asked me "Mama why are you always sitting in the dark". I never answered her. I felt like I just wanted to be in darkness. When I would look into a mirror I almost hated myself because I was so ashamed of what had happened to me. See the devil wants us to think that we have to stay in bondage but we do not have to if we learn how to give it to Jesus. I was not just raped one or two times I was raped five times or more. In the natural it seemed like I would have lost my mind. I will never forget the next rape because the rapist put a knife to my stomach. It was a dark cold night at about four o'clock in the morning. I was out looking for crack I was in a well-populated area too. I was walking past this alley when out of nowhere this man grabbed me and he drug me into the alley. There were houses and apartments all around but no one would help me. I know people were looking because someone eventually called the police. Before that was done however this man threw me to the ground. He got on top of me, he spread my legs apart and he raped me. Then he held my head and tried to put his penis in my mouth. I remember holding my mouth so tight to keep him from putting his penis in my mouth. I began to fight for my life that night in that dark alley. I mean I fought and I fought. I guess the man was going to kill me too so I could not tell on him. So he took the knife he had and he tried to cut my throat. I grabbed the knife with my bare hands and blocked it from my throat. He was stronger than I was so he kept trying to cut to get to my throat. The knife sliced into my hands while I struggled with him and blood was everywhere. He put huge gashes in my hands. Finally the police made it to the scene and they immediately took me to a hospital. When I arrived at the hospital, the doctors there immediately performed surgery on my hands. They did all they could do so I would not lose the use of them all together. They saved my hands but I had some major nerves and ligaments severed that left my hands permanently disabled.

I thank God for doctors because they did a very good job of saving my hands. On one of my hands my middle finger is paralyzed to where it sticks up like I am giving the finger all the time. Sometimes when I am talking to people they took at me strange if I use a hand gesture to explain something. It is so funny sometimes. I remember this one time I was up giving a testimony in church and I told about how my hands got injured. I said to the congregation "I'm not flipping all off it's just that my hands are stuck this way." I held my hand to the congregation to let them see. If someone had walked in the room at that moment they would have sworn I was giving the whole church the finger. Later one of my friends who was there told me how funny that was. She said she was in the back crunched over from laughter. She said it did look like I was flipping everybody off while I was saying "praise you Jesus." We laugh at that all the time. Even though my hands are dead in the natural I can still use them by God's supernatural power and I thank God for being alive today.

My fifth rape was a result of me being at the wrong place at the wrong time. I was trying to get high and this guy took advantage of the whole situation and raped me. I didn't leave after he did it either I stayed and got high with him. I was truly messed up. I talk about this rape in another chapter in this book.

I share these stories because I know that there are women who have been through similar situations and raped. I would just like to speak an encouraging word to you. The enemy wants to keep you feeling like you are nobody but I want you to know that you are somebody in God. You do not have to stay in bondage after you have been raped. It is not your fault the men are just sick or on drugs. I am actually saying today that God has given me love where there has been hate. He has given me peace when there was no peace and joy when there was no joy. He gave me rest when I had sleepless nights. I can say today that I had to let go and let God and I had to forgive my rapists. The bible say in Mark 11:26 "But if you do not forgive, neither will your father who is in heaven forgive your trespasses". I thank God because it took God to heal me from the inside and outside. That is why I say this was my deepest and darkest fear because now I have no more fear.

One thing I have learned is you have to face your fears to overcome them. The bible says that "He will keep us in perfect peace if we keep our minds on him". (Isaiah 26:3) I am not tormented anymore by my rapists. I have turned my whole life over to God. The bible is like a map that directs you into all the right paths. I can truly say without a doubt that I can look into the mirror and love myself and my enemies. Today I will look back and know it was nobody but God because I can say that I love men today. I can say that I am not scared anymore and I thank God for the victory. I do not let anybody tell me that I am nothing. God gave me back everything that the rapists took from me. He gave me pride, dignity, and self-esteem, yes God gave it all back. That is why I say today we do not have to hang our heads down. God says we are somebody. I am saved today and living for God. I have fellowshipped with him and I am so excited about what God is doing in my life. What He has done for me He can do it for you. I was a backslider and I know that I needed God back in my life to help me through this darkness that I was in. I thank God for deliverance. When the devil tried to get me down I tell the devil he is a liar. The bible says I am a new creature in Christ. The old things are passed away and behold all things are become new. (II Corinthians 5:17) My past is under the blood. I thank God today for the blood because it washes me white as snow. No matter how I washed and scrubbed when I was raped I could never get clean. The blood however cleans us that is why I can stand up and tell anybody that has been raped God can clear you up and turn your life around. We can say with boldness "I am loved". "I am a beautiful woman and I am somebody". I am no longer rape minded but I am God minded. I keep my mind on God because the bible says if I do he will keep me in perfect peace. I am not in darkness anymore but I am in the light because Christ is in me. The bible says in

Philippians 4:8 "whatsoever things are just, whatsoever things are pure, whatsoever things are lovely and whatsoever things are of a good report think on those things. I think on those things because if I let the devil get in my mind he will get in my spirit. The devil hates when we get the victory over our lives. That is why I say let go and let God. I am victorious and I am an over comer. I am a mighty woman of God today. God has given me a passion for women that has been raped. See God is a good God and a merciful God. What the devil tried to destroy God cleaned it up for his good. That is why I praise God so much. There is power in God and prayer. Prayer changes things. I am a living witness that it will. I guarantee if you lean on God and trust in Jesus the deepest darkest fear of your life will have to let go of you in Jesus name. There is power in the blood of Jesus. I was torn up from the floor up but Jesus picked me up. He had to reach way down but he picked me up. Today I have victory in my mind. Colossians 3:2 says "I set my mind on the things above not on the things on the earth. I set my mind in the things of God. Philippians 4:7 says "the peace of God which passes all understanding keeps my heart and mind through Christ Jesus.

The bible says as the man thinks in his heart so is he. (Proverbs 23:7) That is why we cannot dwell on the past. Our words are very powerful because life and death are in the power of the tongue. That is why I speak life into my circumstances. We have a choice and today I choose to be free from my rapists. I am no longer in bondage. I have called all of my body parts back from my rapists in the name of Jesus. God has restored me in a mighty, mighty way. I have so much joy right now! I cannot help but thank God for the blood. If it had not been for Jesus dying on the cross for me where would I be today? Because he died and rose from the dead I am totally set free from the bondage that the devil thought he had me bound to. God wants us happy and that I am. I am I have overcome by his blood. I walk in the light of God today. I am no longer in darkness. He is the light and His blood cleanses me. I will praise the Lord with my whole heart. I have a right to. He has been mighty good to me. Ephesians 2:13 says "I was once afar off but now I have been brought near by the blood of Christ. Hebrews 4:16 says "by His blood I have obtained mercy and grace that I may come boldly to God's throne. Well this is part of my testimony as a rape victim and this is how I overcame my rapes and now I am a minister in church and on the streets. I share my testimony with rape victims and anyone else who has an addiction. I share this with love and compassion. For the bible says "If you have not love everything you do is in vain". (I Corinthians 13) I thank God for the love He has put in my heart. This is my prayer for you that God will touch your mind and heal you inside and out, in Jesus Name.

X

Prison Time

I USED TO sell crack to support my addiction and like I have said before I was my own best customer. One day I was out selling crack and I sold to an undercover narcotics officer. We call them narcs. I did not know the man was an undercover agent because he was with one of my friends. She knew he was a narc yet she did not let me know it. She was probably in some kind of trouble and was cooperating with the police to get off some charges or something. I know because I have done it before myself. Well I wound up selling the officer some drugs and I didn't think much more about it. Later on that night I had gone home and went to bed. I was sleeping soundly when I was awakened by someone kicking in the door. It was the narcs. There were so many of them it was like they were everywhere. They grabbed me and told me to get dressed because I was under arrest. They interrogated me and tried to get me to tell them who were my suppliers. I was not about to tell them anything. Hey, I was no snitch. I would rather do jail time than to snitch on someone. Like I said before in this book, if you want to get yourself killed real fast just be a snitch. After I was taken to jail I stayed there forty days and then I was released. The terms of my release were I was placed under supervised probation. This meant I had to report once a month to a probation officer and have a urine test to see if I was using drugs or not. I could not be arrested and I could not keep company with anyone who was a felon. I managed to stay out of trouble but I was dirty a few times when I took a urine test. This caused my probation officer and me not to get along at all. As a result I stayed in court all the time trying not to be charged with parole violation. I argued with my probation officer so much that my daughter had to be assigned to mediate for me. When we went to court anything I had to say I would tell her and she would relay the message. I was still and addict even though I was on supervised probation. I guess the probation just made getting high more of a challenge. I remember my third husband had this television set that we used to pawn when we did not have any money to get high with. The pawn shop probably had seen that TV about twenty times or more. One day I decided to pawn the TV without my husband. I thought it would be okay since we had done it so many times before. Well when he found out what I had done he was ticked off. I knew my husband didn't give a flip about that TV. He was just mad because he did not get a chance to smoke up the money from it with me. My husband then pulled a dirty move. He had me arrested for stealing his TV. Now how do you like that? This man was impossible. I stayed in jail for a few months behind his accusation. This was what caused me to eventually go to prison. If he had not pressed charges against me I would not have gone to prison. When I confronted him about having me arrested he lied and said he had dropped the charges but he didn't. I thought I was in the clear but because my husband did not drop the charges the state prosecuting attorney picked up the case. Since I was on probation this was filed as a parole violation. My parole officer probably was glad to sign off on me because we did not like each other anyway. Not too much longer after I had been released this time the police came looking for me. I remember I was at home and when I saw them headed towards the house I ran and hid in the closet. My husband was home with me and I thought he was going to cover for me. He spilled it all and told them that I was hiding in the closet. I should have known he would rat me out after all he was the one who had me arrested in the first place. I was taken to jail again and this time I was sentenced to two years prison. I remember years before all this had happened, a woman of God had ministered to me on the streets and she told me I would wind up in prison. She told me I needed to turn from the life I was living. She told me that God wanted to use me to help other addicts. She didn't know I used to be a pastor's wife prior to my crack addiction. She said if I didn't heed her warning I would be incarcerated and I would preach the gospel to the other inmates. She also said I would one day be a great evangelist. I didn't listen to the "word" that the woman of God gave me. I liked getting high too much to listen to her warning. I thought I knew it all. Nobody could tell me anything. I was disobedient and stubborn so five years later I wound up in prison just like she had prophesied. The day I went to prison was one of the worst days of my life. I remember this huge metal gate that stood at the prison entrance. There were fences everywhere and security cameras all over the place. As I walked through the main entrance of the prison I could hear the doors close behind me. I began to cry. Prison has a psychological effect on you. When you hear that gate close you know then that you are not getting out until your time is up. I was crying and feeling sorry for myself when I heard God's voice within me just as clear as if He were standing right in front of me. He said "Shut up Myra! I gave you warning after warning and chance after chance". I didn't know how to react to those words. I knew it was the truth. All my deceitful ways had finally caught up with me. It was at that moment that I had a sobering epiphany. I could either remain in self-pity or die inside, or I could stand strong and let God change the things about me that I didn't like. I started to remember the scriptures that I had learned in the ministry like I John 1:9 which says, if we confess our sins, God is faithful and just to forgive us and cleanse us of all unrighteousness. I knew I needed a serious cleansing. Other scriptures began to come to me like Romans 8:1, there is no condemnation to those who are in Christ Jesus, who walk not after the flesh, but after the Spirit. I recognized Jesus as the master of my life not crack. I realized the blood of Jesus paid the penalty for my sin but I still would suffer the consequences of what I had done. After I had my moment I stopped crying and repented of my sin. I clung to what the Word of God said and now I am a new creature in Christ. During my prison stay God did use me. I used to minister to the inmates when the prison did not have a speaker for Sunday service. I loved to praise God and I wanted to share with them what God was doing in my life. I would get so excited with my praise that I would get written up sometimes. They would put me on code silent. That was a punishment of total silence and no activity during church. I was never able to completely follow those rules because whenever the word went forth I started worshiping God. I would throw my hands up and I would jump up and shout hallelujah without even thinking about it. I would say thank you Jesus to any inspirational word the preacher gave even though I knew I would get into trouble. I praised God and I had a right to praise Him. No one knew how good God had been to me. Even though I was locked up I had joy in my heart because it was the beginning of a new chapter of my life. A happy chapter full of hope and success. I left my crack addiction and my old way of life and I have never looked back.

XI

Bad Relationships

AS AN ADDICT I dated many different men. I brought these men in and out of my children's lives. Most of the relationships were like my marriages crazy and abusive. I remember this one man I dated who was a real psycho. I mean he was just nuts and I must have been nuts too because I kept hooking up with him. I broke up with him several times because he was the crazy jealous type but somehow we always managed to get back together. I remember after I broke up with him the first time he would basically stalk me. I had taken this trick to my house one night and he followed me to see what I was going to do. He stood outside the house and demanded that I come out because he said I was his woman and if he could not have me no one else would have me either. The trick I was with knew this man had issues. He did not want to get involved in our drama so he left. My ex then bombarded the house and grabbed me. He had a can of gasoline in his hands. I got away from him and ran into the bedroom and closed the door. I knew he was crazy but I just did not know how crazy. He then kicked the door in and doused me with gasoline. It got all over the room and saturated me and the bed. My ex started talking real crazy. He asked me "Why do you hurt me so much". He said he loved me and I was the only woman for him. I did not respond to him so he took a match out of his pocket and lit it. I did not really think he would set me on fire. I thought he just wanted to give me a good scare because that was the kind of relationship we had, yeah it was sick. Well that nut was not bluffing that night. He threw the match on the floor and ran out of the room. I jumped up and moved so the fire would not spread and hit me. I was screaming and praying all at the same time. While this transpiring man's son just so happened to come by at that very moment. When he saw the fire and heard me screaming he rushed in and rescued me. He immediately put the fire out because he did not want his dad to get into any kind of incriminating trouble. I was so shaken up by everything that I was trembling. The man's son was a drug dealer so he offered me some crack to calm my nerves. He didn't really care about me; he was just trying to make things right for his dad. He said "don't worry about my dad, I got what you need right here". I did need a big hit after that ordeal so I took a hit to sooth my nerves. I got high then I soon forgot about the severity of what my ex had done. I did not care that he tried to burn me alive I was just happy to get some free crack. I got so sprung that it was like I was in a crack paradise. Later that same night my ex returned to my house and I got high with him too. I did not have enough sense to realize how dangerous this man was but I did learn it in the end. After I finished getting high I went to the police station to tell them what my ex had done. They wanted me to fill out a complaint form to press charges and I had to pay six or seven dollars to have it processed. I was outraged. How dare they ask me for seven dollars that was like asking for a thousand. I needed all my money to buy crack. I decided not to press charges because crack was more important to me than getting a psycho off the streets. I went to the crack house instead.

After that incident this ex-boyfriend really thought he had me right where he wanted me. I remember we got into an argument because I was living with this man who was disabled. He was a trick and since I had nowhere to live after the psycho burned my house this man let me stay with him. My ex was jealous of every man that I associated with. It did not matter who it was he was just that crazy. One time he got drunk and strangled me out of a fit of jealous rage. He choked me within an inch of my life. When I came to I was in the hospital emergency room. He could have killed me. I guess we got a rush out of living life on the edge. Well, let me go back to the night we had the argument. My ex told me he was tired of chasing behind me. I blew him off because I did not want him nor did I care about his jealousy. He had an iron cane in his hand so he took the cane and hit me with it. I began to curse at him and call him names. The trick I was living with tried to help me but he could not do anything because he was old and disabled. My ex beat me with that cane and beat me until he was tired. He broke both of my arms and both of my legs. He beat me unconscious. The trick called the paramedics and when I came to I was in the hospital emergency room again. We were both crazy crack addicts and all the abuse I took from him was still not enough to make me stop smoking crack.

After this craziness went on so long my ex and I got back together again and tried to make things work. We wanted to get clean so we began to attend church. We called ourselves delivered but really we were not. We started this support group at the church called "Addicts on a Mission".

We ministered to many addicts with this group but they did not get free. I found that since we called ourselves addicts we remained addicts and could not break free. I remember I would even go to the meetings ministering to the other addict while I was high. I asked God "Why can't I stop getting high?" That is when God revealed to me that I was still in bondage and I had to stop confessing what I did not want to be or to have in my life. Everyone in that group stayed in bondage because ironically as it may sound we really were addict on a mission. Our mission was to get money and sympathy to get high. In my heart I was really sincere. I wanted to be delivered but I was confessing addiction. What I was confessing is what took over me and I could not get delivered.

When "Addicts on a Mission" started there was a big write up about it in the local newspaper. I remember I used to go to the courthouse with the addicts and the judges would use me as a mentor and an example of success. These addicts were members of "Addicts on a Mission". Little did they know I was still smoking crack. I felt like a traitor inside over all the deception. I did not know if I could keep up who I was pretending to be. Crack made me very sneaky. Everyone was so proud of me because they knew my past and they figured if "California" could get delivered then there was hope for everybody. I cannot lie I was one of the worst addict you could have ever encountered. I brought the California style of crack addiction to the country in Arkansas. That is how I got the name "California". I was no joke either. I used to pimp men and women. I would make girls turn my tricks for me. I would steal a person's dope and then sell them back their own dope. Now that I am truly delivered it is hard for people to believe I have changed. Sometimes when people know your past it is hard for them to see you for what you are. They seem to want to remember you the way you were. You need to avoid people who want to keep you where you were. I have this friend whose husband knew me when I was an addict. He made a joke about me to her one day. He said "You'd better watch out for Myra because if you keep hanging around her the next thing you know she'll have you on the street corner working for her". We both laugh at that now because one day we were out on the street ministering and she was standing on the corner winning souls for Christ when I said to her, "Well I guess your husband was right about me having you on the street corner because here you are on the corner working". Oh, if we didn't laugh and laugh at that. My friend only knows me as the delivered Myra and she knows I am sold out for Jesus. She is the one who wrote my story for me and helped me organize my thoughts for this book.

I remember when I wanted to be delivered so badly. I had this burning desire in me to come out of the bondage I was in. I had finally come to the point where I was tired of myself and tired of crack. I would be at the crack house talking about Jesus while I was all doped up. Even though I was an addict God still used me to prophesy to the other addicts. I wanted to get high one time and God wanted me to give a word to this young lady that was smoking with me. God weighed so heavy on my heart that I could not get high until I told this girl what He wanted her to know. When they say God works in mysterious ways you better believe he does. I told the girl that God was going to restore her marriage and her money that she had lost. I told her it was going to happen in two days. Well it came to pass just like I had prophesied to her. After that she got delivered and stopped smoking crack. She gave her testimony to me and others. She told me I did not belong in the crack house. As a matter of fact many times in my life addicts have told me that. Well now I am out of the crack house. I have been clean for seven years and I will never go back. I can now minister and prophesy to people and God uses me in that area. I praise God that he did not give up one me. Well I eventually left the violent, psycho guy who was so jealous. I had to learn that when a person really loves you there is no abuse involved. It was a hard lesson to learn too.

XII

The Power to Overcome

WHAT A MIGHTY, mighty God we serve I know He is mighty because He has shown His power through my life. Some experts say you can't be free from addiction but look at me. I am totally free. This is a message to all the psychologists, psychiatrists, counselors, teachers, ministers, and people who falsely assume that once you are addicted that you will remain that way for life. Some say you will crave the drug and you have to fight that desire for it every day. Some even say you have to constantly stay busy to get your mind off of the drug. Well that is a lie straight from the pit of hell. I am a living witness here to tell you that "whom the sun sets free is free indeed". I am totally delivered. I am totally healed and I am totally cleansed from my former life and lifestyle. God has given me peace and I don't desire crack or any other drug. I can talk about the former addiction and share my testimony with no problem. I have no desire to go back to crack. The addiction has no power over me. I am in control by the power of God. Now don't get me wrong, I'm not telling you that I am going to go sit in the crack house and be foolish. I am saying if drugs were presented to me now I have more God in me than desire for crack. I knew this Man who had gotten off crack. He was clean and he began to preach. He would come from time to time to witness to a group of us at the crack house. He would talk to us about how we can be clean like him. He'd tell us about God and how we needed to give our lives to Jesus to get off crack. Well after coming to the crack house so much the influence started to take its toll on him. Before we knew anything that preacher was smoking again. See, he was not totally delivered he was just away from the crowd. When he got the opportunity to go back what was inside of him took over. To overcome crack a person has to be delivered and under the blood. It takes the power of God to minister to crack addicts especially if you are a former addict yourself. Like I said I have more God in me than I have desire for crack. When you are delivered the anointing has destroyed every yoke. God does not just break the spirit of bondage he destroys it because bondage is the sprit that drives the crack addiction. God is the God of the impossible. He does nothing half-way. He completes whatever He does. Whatever He says in His word that is exactly what He will do. I am a living witness that He WILL do just what he says. I am so glad to share this testimony because I want everyone to know "You can be free"! The devil does not want you to know the truth. He does not want you to gain any victory over your situation. The devil wants to keep you bound. He wants you to believe his lie that there is no hope. Well to bad devil, there is hope for the addict. That's why I continually praise God. I have been through things many people could not endure yet God held me together. I continually praise Him. Behind all of my tears there is a story to tell. That is why I keep my testimony real. I stress that it has to be real because I want people to know there is someone who has been through the same thing they are going through. I was right there stuck and addicted for nineteen years. Sometimes the enemy will come and bring my past to my remembrance. He tries to make me feel condemned and ashamed. That is one of the tactics he uses to get people to stop trying and give up. He wants you to remain where you are but I am here to tell you to never give up. God can take a prostitute from the street and make her a respected housewife. He can take a whoremongering "crack head" and make him a respectable husband. He can make you a mighty man or woman of God. I am a living witness. I am clean and under the blood. I minister to people and do evangelistic work. Our God is patient and kind. He never gave up on me even when I was immersed in a life of sin getting high on crack. Now I have a supernatural high not a crack high. I don't have to pay money for this high. I don't have to stand on the street corners and sell my body for this high. Neither do I have to steal and rob for this high. Praise God all I had to do was accept Jesus Christ as my personal Savior. By that I mean I had to repent and turn away from sin. The bible says you must not be lukewarm or God will spew you out of His mouth. (Revelation 3:16) You have to sell out one hundred percent to God and that is what has happened to me. I have lost my old mind and now I have the mind of Christ. I am so glad the scripture say God is not a man that He should lay. (Numbers 23:19) That is His character and His word. I am excited to share these different accounts of my life so everyone can know how God works. He can bring us out of any mess. Jesus' death was not in vain. He died for us all to have eternal life. We have the right to use his name today. All hell trembles at the name of Jesus. We are not predestined to be addicts. God knows everything we have done and everything we will do. God does not force his will on anybody. He gives us a choice to make He said in Deuteronomy 30:15, I set before your life and death blessing and cursing, choose life that you may live. I made the choice to use crack. That was not God. He predestined me for His work not for me to serve the devil. Crack addiction was never in His divine plan. Now that I understand God's will for my life I can't stop praising Him and thanking Him for his goodness and mercy. I serve Him as fervently as I served that crack pipe. I renew my mind daily with the word of God. As a result God has given me the power to overcome any addiction. Praise is to God. If it had not been for Him I know I would be dead. He gave me a second chance. Not only did He give me a second chance but He also gave my sisters and brothers a second change as well. We used to get high together and we would fight and fight over crack. They used to get mad at me because I would always be the one with the most crack. I remember I used to taunt them by smoking in their face when their crack had run out. One time my brother knocked a crack pipe out of my hand because he was so angry. Now my siblings can watch me praise the Lord. I only mention them in this book to let you know that no matter how powerful crack is God is more powerful. I get excited when I look in the mirror and see what God has done in my life. God has been better to me than I could ever have been to myself. Whenever I think about Him, I am truly grateful. The type of life I was living was horrible but God kept His angels encamped around me so that I would not go down into the pit. The enemy could not take me out, Hallelujah. God gave me a new beginning. That is the kind of God He is. I am so blessed that neither of my daughters became addicts. I know God's hand was on them too. I have had many associates that did drugs with me and their children are now smoking like them. My daughters did not follow in my footsteps. You have to recognize generational curses and they have to be broken from the lives or you children. The blood of Jesus is more powerful than any curse. I am mentioning my daughters because I want you to understand how powerful God is. One of my girls is a sergeant at a prison facility the other one is a registered nurse. My grandchildren often talk about pursuing professional occupations as well. I believe they will achieve more than their moms. As a matter of fact, I know they will because they have a praying grandmother and I have learned to command the devil in the name of Jesus to take his hands off their lives. God has blessed me with a new beginning and the blessing is extended to my family. I am determined to remain delivered from crack cocaine. The scripture says I can do all things through Jesus Christ who strengthens me. (Philippians 3:16) I have supernatural strength and supernatural ability. Today I am saved, sanctified, and filled with the Holy Spirit. I refuse to bow down to the enemy. I tell my testimony to strengthen you to refuse to bow down too. I thank God for a mind to stay delivered. I confess that I will never be an addict again. God has washed me, and cleansed me, and made me as white as snow. God is using me now to minister to people on the streets. I have been drug free for seven year and for me there is no turning back. I have a new addition and His name is Jesus. The first step to deliverance is to accept Jesus Christ as your personal Savior. Romans 10:9 says that if you confess with your mouth that Jesus is Lord and believe in your heart that God has raised Him from the dead, then you will be saved. For with the heart men believe unto righteousness and with the mouth confession is made unto salvation. The next step is to receive the Holy Ghost who gives us the power. Acts 1:8 says, but you shall receive power, after that the Holy Ghost is come upon you: and you shall be witnesses unto me both in Jerusalem, and in all Judea, and in Samaria and unto the uttermost part of the earth. The third step to deliverance is to find a good church where the anointing is flowing. I attend Full Counsel Church in Pine Bluff, Arkansas. It is a spirit filled, anointed church that has a pastor who does not sugar coat the word. It is the anointing that destroys the yoke. It is located at 517 South Cherry Street. The people you associate with and the words you hear continually will make a difference in your mindset. Whatever you think about most is what you will do and become. Proverbs 23:7 says, as a man thinks in his heart so is he. I have to renew my mind daily to stay free. It is not a struggle but it is a commitment and a choice.

'CALIFORNIA'

ADDICTED

NO HOPE

Edwards Brothers Malloy
Thorofare, NJ USA
May 2, 2013